Scientific Publishing

T0348641

CHANDOS
INFORMATION PROFESSIONAL SERIES

Series Editor: Ruth Rikowski
(e-mail: Rikowskigr@aol.com)

Chandos' new series of books are aimed at the busy information professional. They have been specially commissioned to provide the reader with an authoritative view of current thinking. They are designed to provide easy-to-read and (most importantly) practical coverage of topics that are of interest to librarians and other information professionals. If you would like a full listing of current and forthcoming titles, please visit our website www.chandospublishing.com or e-mail info@chandospublishing.com or telephone +44 (0) 1223 891358.

New authors: we are always pleased to receive ideas for new titles; if you would like to write a book for Chandos, please contact Dr Glyn Jones on e-mail gjones@chandospublishing.com or telephone number +44 (0) 1993 848726.

Bulk orders: some organisations buy a number of copies of our books. If you are interested in doing this, we would be pleased to discuss a discount. Please e-mail info@chandospublishing.com or telephone +44 (0) 1223 891358.

Scientific Publishing:
From vanity to strategy

HANS E. ROOSENDAAL,
KASIA ZALEWSKA-KUREK,
PETER A.TH.M. GEURTS
AND
EBERHARD R. HILF

Chandos Publishing

Oxford · Cambridge · New Delhi

Chandos Publishing
TBAC Business Centre
Avenue 4
Station Lane
Witney
Oxford OX28 4BN
UK
Tel: +44 (0) 1993 848726
E-mail: info@chandospublishing.com
www.chandospublishing.com

Chandos Publishing is an imprint of Woodhead Publishing Limited

Woodhead Publishing Limited
Abington Hall
Granta Park
Great Abington
Cambridge CB21 6AH
UK
www.woodheadpublishing.com

First published in 2010

ISBN:
978 1 84334 490 2

© Hans E. Roosendaal, Kasia Zalewska-Kurek, Peter A.Th.M. Geurts
and Eberhard R. Hilf, 2010

Typeset in the UK by Concerto.

Contents

List of tables and figures

Tables

Figures

About the authors

Hans E. Roosendaal is professor of strategic management at the University of Twente in the Netherlands. His specialisation is in strategic knowledge and information management.

Educated as a physicist, in 1974 he joined the University of Bielefeld (Germany) as faculty staff. Between 1983 and 1998 he served Elsevier Science in various management positions as publisher and in corporate strategy and acquisitions. He joined the University of Twente in 1998 as chief information officer, and has also served as a member of the executive board of the university.

He has authored journal and book articles on both surface physics and scientific information. The articles on scientific information focus on strategic aspects of the transformation to a digital environment.

Hans is chairman of the Foundation natuurkunde.nl, a foundation supported by the Dutch physics community with the aim of making physics more attractive to young people. To this end, the foundation operates two websites: www.natuurkunde.nl and www.sciencespace.nl.

He served on a number of evaluation committees on digital libraries, e-science and e-learning, and from 2004 to 2008 was a member of the BMBF standing evaluation committee on D-Grid. Since 2006 he has been a member of the Standing Accreditation Committee of the Zentrale Evaluations- und Akkreditierungsagentur, Hannover, Germany.

Kasia Zalewska-Kurek is assistant professor at the University of Twente in the Netherlands. She holds a master's degree in sociology from the University of Wroclaw, Poland, and has specialised in the sociology of small urban and rural communities. Her master's thesis dealt with the quality of life in a small town, describing relations between the perceived quality of life and a number of external influences such as economic, cultural and social factors (derived from Manuel Castells's theory of urban subsystems).

In 2004 she joined the University of Twente to pursue a PhD, and in 2008 defended her dissertation, entitled 'Strategies in the production and dissemination of knowledge'. The dissertation answers questions on the dynamics of and conditions affecting the production of knowledge; it also applies the concept of the business model to the research environment.

Her research interest is in the strategic management and organisation of scientific research: in the research process, including production and transfer of knowledge, and in the management of research institutes and universities. She has co-authored articles and a book chapter on the management of the production of knowledge and scientific information.

Peter A.Th.M. Geurts is associate professor for research methods and methodology of the social sciences at the University of Twente in the Netherlands. He specialises in survey methods at large, and more specifically in such methods in the context of contingent valuation and international comparisons. Educated in mathematical sociology, he joined the University of Twente as faculty staff responsible for the teaching of research methods in public administration.

He has authored books on methodological issues concerning questionnaire construction and research proposals, and books and journal articles on scientific information, mixed methods, contingent valuation of welfare change and issues of social and political participation in democracies.

Since the beginning of the 1990s he has conducted and published several studies on the impact of ICT, more specifically the internet, on publishing models in science and developments in scientific and business communication. His primary concern here is the theoretical and empirical underpinning of the transitions taking place under the influence of the internet.

Peter is a member of advisory committees for research grants of the Netherlands Organisation for Scientific Research (NWO) and a reviewer for several scientific journals.

Eberhard R. Hilf is CEO of the Institute for Science Networking Oldenburg associated with the Carl von Ossietzky University. The institute works on innovative services for the management of scientific information in the digital age.

Eberhard's interests are digital scientific publication services: refereeing, printing on demand, metadata, distribution, networking and semantic analysis, with open access as a prerequisite.

Educated as a theoretical physicist (Hamburg, Munich, Berlin and Frankfurt), he was a research assistant at the University of Würzburg and professor at the Universities of Düsseldorf, Darmstadt and Oldenburg, with sabbaticals at

Seattle, Jerusalem, New York and Orsay/Paris. He has organised many scientific conferences in both physics and science information management.

Eberhard was on the scientific advisory boards for HAL, the CNRS Central Archive, the National Data-Centre FIZ Karlsruhe, the National Networking of Chemistry e-Learning and the Virtual Scientific Library ViFaPhys (Technical Information Library TIB Hannover), and a member of the Action Committee for Publication and Scientific Communication (EPS European Physical Society).

He has served in the DINI German Initiative for Network Information, and co-founded and chaired the IuK Initiative for Information and Communication of the German Learned Societies, and the Action Group for the reform of the Urheberrechtsgesetz for science and academic learning.

List of acronyms

AAAS	American Association for the Advancement of Science
ACP	*Atmospheric Chemistry and Physics*
CERN	European Organization for Nuclear Research
DFG	Deutsche Forschungsgemeinschaft (German Research Foundation)
FTE	full-time equivalent
IR	institutional repository
IT	information technology
NARCIS	National Academic Research and Collaborations Information System (Netherlands)
NWO	Netherlands Organisation for Scientific Research
NSF	US National Science Foundation
OA	organisational autonomy
OAI	Open Archives Initiative
R&D	research and development
R&HE	research and higher education
RAID	redundant array of independent disks

ROAR	Registry of Open Access Repositories
ROC	receiver operating characteristic
SI	strategic interdependence
UNESCO	UN Economic, Scientific and Cultural Organization

About this book

This book presents an overview of the literature on developments in scientific publishing over roughly the last decade, viewed from the perspective of how scientific publishing can serve research while research also develops over time. A relevant and recent driving force for these developments is information technology.

The book attempts to address a broader audience of university, library and research managers, policy-makers, publishers, researchers and students in research management and information sciences, and all those who are intellectually interested in and challenged by cultural change in the dynamics of science.

Chapter 1 provides an introduction to the subject and a rationale for the approach taken. Chapters 2–5 provide detailed analyses of the use of business models in research, the research environment and the acquisition of scientific information, before turning to a detailed description of the market for scientific information. A synthesis of these findings is then given in Chapter 6, discussing criteria for business models in scientific publishing, and in Chapter 7, sketching scenarios. This is followed by an analysis of the consequences these findings bear for the various stakeholders in Chapter 8. Chapter 9 provides a summary and overall conclusions.

Readers primarily interested in the managerial aspects of scientific publishing may want to read in particular Chapters 1 and 6–9, while turning to Chapters 2–5 to find a detailed underpinning of the arguments used. Readers mainly interested in the dynamics of science may like to read Chapters 1–5, while readers who want to enjoy the full menu of how these dynamics impact on scientific publishing are advised to consult the entire book.

All web links in the references and throughout the book were checked and found to be working on 24 May 2009. All links given in the references and throughout the book can be accessed online at *http://www.isn-oldenburg.de/~hilf/publications/scientific-publishing-from-vanity-to-strategy.html*, which page will be regularly checked and updated by the authors.

1

Introduction

Why this book, why this book now and why this subtitle? These seem valid questions, as recently quite a number of books have been published on publishing, and in particular scientific publishing (Cope and Philips, 2006, 2009; Kist, 2008). Most of these books deal with changes in technology and their consequences for scientific publishing and archiving, as we have seen these over the past decade. In this book we take a different approach, albeit that we also take technological changes as our starting point. However, the purpose is not to analyse changes in publishing, but first to analyse what these technology changes mean for doing science, i.e. for the research process as it has developed and will further develop as e-science. E-science will no doubt enhance science; one could argue that e-science also stands for enhanced science.[1] The consequences for scientific publishing will be discussed on the basis of this analysis of the changes in science and in the research process in particular.

In a previous book (Roosendaal et al., 2005) we formulated a vision for the scientific information market, a vision that according to the present authors still holds today:

> The research and higher education information market will in future be based on a network of information relating to research and education that conform to

> open standards, and an accommodating architecture that allows users the easiest and fastest possible access to this information.
>
> The information available by such a network will not only comprise of information material for research and higher education, but also of management information relating to this information.
>
> The market is the research and higher education community. This network will be an open and global network.

In the scientific community, this vision is generally shared. It describes in essence an information network for research and education. This network should contain both research and education information in the widest sense. This means also management information to support access to and disclosure of the information. The user, student, teacher or researcher should be able to make use of this information from any site, at any time and in all possible ways. And the network should allow the user to integrate the information into his or her daily working processes.

This universal vision has driven and will continue to drive the market for research and higher education information and, as a consequence, the business models in this market. Engines for change supporting better fulfilment of this vision have always triggered and will continue to trigger changes in the business model.

E-science is seen as a further step towards the all-time ideal of universal sharing of scientific results. What kind of incentives will be required to attain this goal of making research information an ever more integral part of the research process? Back in the 1990s there was already some speculation on the consequences for the research process of what we now call e-science or cyber-science. It was widely speculated that e-science, the term we will use throughout this book, could increase the turnover rate of science to make the process more effective and efficient. Such an increase is badly needed, given the fact that for more than three centuries the productivity per scientist has not increased while at the same time most countries, except for China and India, have exhausted the full potential in the population that can reasonably be expected to enjoy higher education. And higher education is a necessary condition in the training of a scientist. Moreover, China and India will exhaust their potential pretty soon as well. This means that if we just want to prolong the present rate of knowledge production, and this is what our present society seems to require, we need to find ways to increase the productivity per scientist – taking into account that, in particular in the production of knowledge, the law of diminishing returns applies mercilessly. One way of increasing the capacity for the production of knowledge is to reduce redundancies in the research process. To attain this requires more efficient and more transparent communication of research results. Also, if the number of multiples (Merton, 1973), i.e. the almost simultaneous inventions by disparate researchers and not resulting from imitation or plagiarism, could be reduced by improved communication, substantial research capacity could possibly be freed, resulting in higher productivity per researcher. And as we are witnessing already today, e-science is an important driver to boost interdisciplinary research, and interdisciplinary research is probably the most important source for the production of new knowledge. Nanoscience may serve as a non-exhaustive example here.

These are just a few of the many good reasons to explore the possibilities e-science has to offer us. The gist is that e-science is a further step in making research information the integral raw material in the research process, as it should be.

In e-science it will be possible to share primary data much more efficiently with other researchers, allowing for new schemes of division of labour, e.g. splitting up collecting data in an advanced way from analysing these same data and so on, as is daily practice in high-energy physics. A condition, of course, is that we can find innovative ways of giving credit where credit is due, as a necessary incentive for sharing information at such an early phase in the research process. No doubt some sciences will seize the opportunity to become more data driven, as was anticipated for biology by Maddox (1998) and advocated by Popper (1963) for the social sciences to become a mature discipline. We have seen this happening very clearly in the Human Genome Project and other forms of cell biology.

These few examples may illustrate the claim that new technology will not only change the way research results will be reported, but also change the research process next to science itself. However, this is not a new claim. Throughout history we have seen how the possibilities promised by new technology were readily seized by the scientific community to improve the efficacy and efficiency of the research process. A case in point is the invention of the research journal in 1665, made possible by the novel distribution channel provided by the postal services of the seventeenth century. The research journal was badly needed to improve the phasing of the researchers of those days, and led to fundamental changes in the research process of that time. The main function of the journal was to improve communication between researchers to the benefit of all, as it was clear to everyone that science could only flourish by collaboration in sharing results: *do ut des*. Beyond communication, at the same time the journal allowed researchers to claim an invention,[2] a function journals still perform and which has developed into a more formal role as an archive of research articles – the emphasis has shifted from communication required for researchers to remain in phase to more formal registration (Roosendaal et al., 2005).

This development has seduced some to speak about 'vanity publishing', and some publishers may well have built their strategies on this concept. E-science, if living up to its promises, must mark the end of 'vanity publishing' and publishers' strategies; rather, it must develop new research and communication strategies with the goal of improving the production of new knowledge. Researchers will have to develop clear strategies for doing research and collaborating in the research environment with their colleagues, as well as with society at large. Publishing strategies should support and therefore facilitate these researchers' strategies.

Based on this thought, this book will first discuss research using the concept of the business model as guidance to analyse the research environment, competition in research and drivers for making research results public and acquisition of these results by other researchers. This will create the foundation to discuss pertinent criteria for business models in scientific publishing, and to develop scenarios for publishing and their consequences for all stakeholders, researchers, publishers and librarians alike. The book will endeavour to speculate on the consequences for the business model of research and higher education (R&HE) institutions as e-science opens up new possibilities for collaboration in projects across such institutions. In particular, this will create new challenges for smaller and medium-sized institutions to participate in such collaborations. E-science promises new possibilities for the production of knowledge and, as we have seen from the few examples given above, will most probably change our research agenda of the future.

This research agenda is to a great extent determined by the rather delicate relation between research and society at large. This relation is presently in flux, moving towards an increasing intertwinement of research and society. Researchers and practitioners involved in this discussion elaborate on the future roles of university and society in the production of knowledge, and it is obvious that e-science nowadays plays a special part in this discussion. The subject of the production of knowledge has been addressed in a number of papers and journal issues (Hodgkinson, 2001; Leydesdorff and Meyer, 2006). In 1999 Gibbons explicitly raised the need for a new social contract between research and society that would result in mutual interactions and 'socially robust' scientific knowledge production. Some solutions (Leydesdorff and Etzkowitz, 1998; Novotny et al., 2003; Swan et al., 2007) have been proposed and are primarily based on descriptions of the observed relations between research and society.

The basic premise in the relation between society and researcher is that it should create incentives for both parties. At present, three modes of such a relation of researchers and the environment are understood: 'ivory tower' and 'strategic research', known also as Mode1 and Mode2 (Gibbons et al., 1994), and the recently introduced Mode3 (Kurek et al., 2007), the 'research entrepreneur'. Compared to researchers in Mode2, the research entrepreneur is more leveraging in the relation with the societal environment. Research entrepreneurs are directing the environment by creating demand for their scientific products rather than supplying material based on the demand of this environment.

As stated, scientific research is of interest not only to researchers but also to their societal environment. This societal environment plays one of the major roles in setting research policies and research directions. By setting the research directions this environment has a direct impact on scientific knowledge production.

The guiding thought throughout this book will be that scientific publishing is here to serve scientific knowledge production. Stimulating e-science is therefore the challenge for scientific publishing. E-science means a further step in the integration of information into the research process, requiring new strategies and business models for scientific publishing to move away *from vanity to strategy*.

Notes

1 These theories draw on the eScience in Action: Workshop on Knowledge and ICTs held at AWT, Rotterdam, on 22 April 2008. Full details can be found at www.awt.nl/?id=602.
2 See the archives of the Royal Society at the Bodleian Library, Oxford, available at www.ouls.ox.ac.uk/bodley.

2

Business models in the research environment

Following the line of thought developed in the Introduction, our basic premise is that publishing business models should be commensurate with the research environment and should serve research. This is just another way of saying that publishing business models should be commensurate with the business models in the research environment. Throughout this book we will use the common definition for a business: an organisation aiming at the exchange of goods, services or both, generally to raise revenues, though not necessarily. A business model should serve a number of purposes.

- It should create value in its environment (Kurek et al., 2006), in particular in the process at hand, i.e. the production of knowledge.

- It should create a sustainable process. Again, we use the common definition of sustainable: a characteristic of a process, system or state that can be maintained at a commensurate level and in 'perpetuity'. It may be obvious that this condition is particularly relevant for the production of knowledge, which is characterised by a strong legacy, i.e. researchers from future generations build on the knowledge produced by previous generations. As Newton is claimed to have stated after having finished his famous *Principia*, 'if I have seen further it is only by standing on the shoulders of Giants',[1] giving in this way proper credit to these predecessors.

- It should create value for commerce, where commerce is commonly defined as the voluntary exchange of goods, services or both, at a profit or not at a profit. The latter, i.e. at a profit or not, is a strategic choice, although not entirely a free choice if we also want to meet the requirement for a sustainable process. This condition is very applicable in research; as we have noted before, research builds entirely on the voluntary exchange of research results as building blocks to further findings.

Summarising, we can define a business model as the organisation of property (ibid.) and the exchange of property – the property being the knowledge produced by the researcher, and in particular the intellectual property of this researcher, as well as the added value of all other stakeholders in the value chain, such as research institutes, universities, publishers and other intermediaries.

Inspecting the literature, it will become clear that there exists no single definition for a business model agreed by the entire business science community. In the strategic management literature the business model is known as one focusing primarily on value creation (Amit and Zott, 2001). Table 2.1 lists roles of the business model (den Braber, 2008) as given in the literature.

These roles of the business model mean that it constitutes a comprehensive, coherent strategic model 'expressing business logic' or 'linking strategy and operations' (Osterwalder et al., 2005).

Also, there are divergent views on what a business model should actually entail in order to serve the rather general conditions mentioned at the beginning of this chapter. Some

Table 2.1   Proposed roles of the business model and their sources

Proposed role	Source
Analysing, implementing and communicating strategic choices	Shafer et al. (2005)
Telling a good story	Magretta (2002)
Linking strategy and operations	Mäkinen and Seppänen (2007)
Linking of strategic management and entrepreneurship theories of value creation	Amit and Zott (2001)
Focusing device that mediates between technology development and economic value creation	Chesbrough and Rosenbloom (2002)
Conceptual tool that contains a set of elements and their relationships, and allows expression of the business logic of a specific firm	Osterwalder et al. (2005)
Intermediate unit of analysis in managing technological ventures arising from R&D	Mäkinen and Seppänen (2007)
Planning	Magretta (2002)

authors restrict a business model more to the finance-related aspects, whereas others, such as Chesbrough and Rosenbloom (2002), view a business model more as an instrument to create a coherent strategy including these finance-related aspects. As mentioned above, a business model should provide a clear response to the needs with respect to value creation articulated in the market while organising the property of the stakeholders.

The model developed by Chesbrough and Rosenbloom for creating value from innovation is particularly suitable for the discussion at hand, as it converges from the wider general perspective of the value proposition to the resulting finance-related aspects, as seen below. Following the operalisation of Chesbrough and Rosenbloom, any business model should perform the following functions.

- Articulate the value proposition. In scientific publishing, the main value proposition is supporting the production of knowledge by making research results public and sharing these in the research environment. Intellectual property and peer review will be seen as important to this value proposition, and it may be obvious that these issues also need be considered in the light of e-science.

- Clearly define the market segment, i.e. the environment to which the scientific products are addressed. This environment can be exclusively the research environment or just a part of this environment, but could also encompass the wider societal environment. An important question is whether the market segment of e-science will end at the research group, the research institute, the scientific domain, the scientific community or the wider societal environment. This will obviously depend on the relation of the researcher with such an environment.

- Reflect the strategic position of researchers, determining the link between them and the environment – defined as everything outside the research organisation.

- Identify the value chain of the research environment, and the position of the value proposition in this chain and the consequences this has for the stakeholders. Here the position of the R&HE institutions is of relevance.

- Reflect the researchers' competitive strategy. It is well known that there exists fierce competition between researchers and research groups (Merton, 1957), and this may well inhibit sharing of research results, thereby affecting the value proposition as mentioned above. Also, the fear for plagiarism has been observed (Kurek et al., 2006) to be a main inhibition in sharing results without any further conditions.

- Identify revenues, cost structure and profit potential. A clear condition here is that the overall revenues and cost structure need to ensure future operations and maintenance of the system, so as to meet the condition of sustainability.

Serving research is possible only if business models support researchers, being – as users – the main stakeholders in doing research. This makes an understanding of the mechanisms of scientific communication in the research process a requirement in developing a publishing business model. The roles of scientific information in the research process, in particular sharing scientific information, will therefore be discussed before dealing with business models, following the argument that scientific communication and scientific information are at the core of research (ibid.).

As noted before, the value proposition in a publishing business model is sharing scientific information. The premise in this book is that scientific information is an integral part of research. Seen from the viewpoint of the research process, scientific information is not a final product but an intermediary product accepted by the scientific community as being worthy of further scientific effort and scrutiny (Popper, 1963). This means that scientific information is not a goal in itself. The information produced in scientific research is created in order to add value to existing scientific knowledge. This work, however, is only of added value if it is shared. Sharing information is in line with our scientific ethos, according to which science should be universal, implying that nobody should be excluded from it. And scientific knowledge as a common property has to be shared, otherwise it does not exist (Merton, 1973). Therefore, researchers being accountable to the research environment make public their results by means of a scientific publication. The research environment can then attempt to falsify these results in future research (Popper, 1934, 1959) or make productive use of it.

These conditions can be fulfilled only if sharing scientific information is the main purpose of scientific publishing. Sharing information leads us further to the acquisition of scientific information. For researchers, scientific information should be available to serve them in their role not only as authors but also as readers. As authors, researchers want to be recognised in their research environment. This requires availability of the information. At the same time, as readers they want to be able to select scientific information effectively and efficiently and stay up to date with scientific developments. The acquisition of scientific information is thus determined by the availability of the information and the ability of researchers to select this information. For the analysis of scientific publishing, we need then to distinguish its two main components:

- making public research results, resulting in scientific information

- acquiring this scientific information.

Publishing business models should account for these two major drivers in the sharing of scientific information.

Specific access to scientific information (e.g. provided by the institute to which researchers are affiliated) and efficient use of this information create competitive advantage by using the acquired information in research to produce results that will add value to scientific knowledge created in a scientific domain. Researchers claim intellectual property rights because they want to be recognised and gain reputation in their research environment, which is, as we have seen, competitive. Therefore this book will discuss a number of aspects of competition affecting scientific information behaviour.

Summarising, scientific information serves researchers in research and in strategic positioning in their research environment, being part of the wider societal environment. The societal environment is defined as the world outside the researcher at a given level of aggregation, and is thus a dynamic environment and can include other researchers, government and industry.

All these aspects of the research environment need to be accounted for in a publishing business model. For the model to be successful and sustainable in the research environment, it should create value in research. A publishing business model has to support business models in the research environment and therefore has to articulate the value proposition clearly, i.e. production of knowledge by sharing scientific information, and define the audience to which this value is addressed, i.e. the research and possibly the societal environment. To this end, it should enable analysis of what the position of this value is and all aspects determining the creation of this value.

As discussed before, researchers have to publish their results. To do so, they have to acquire scientific information. They need the information to be available anytime, anyhow and anywhere. As the acquisition of scientific information is important for research, it should be facilitated by services provided by business models for scientific publishing. To this end, an analysis of conditions under which scientific research is being performed is required in the first place. Next to this, the efficacy and efficiency of the acquisition of scientific information have to be optimised to allow effective use of this information.

This leads to a set of criteria that publishing business models should account for. These criteria are derived from the analysis of the role of these business models with respect to the business model for research. The main parameters of a publishing business model that will be seen to arise from this analysis are the *availability* of scientific information and the power of *selection*. These parameters will be discussed for a suite of business models, including known publishing models such as the subscription model and the present model to realise open access, a model that we will call for brevity the *open access* model in the remainder of this book.

This book is structured following the guiding principles given by the business model of Chesbrough and Rosenbloom (2002) and making use of the inherent convergence in this model. Starting from the role of business models in the research environment, characteristics of this environment relevant to publishing business models have been discussed in this chapter. This flows naturally into a discussion of the strategic positioning of researchers, as scientific information is a determinant to this strategic positioning. Strategic positioning means competition, in both research and societal environments, resulting in consequences for competition in scientific information, both in making research results public and in acquiring scientific information.

All these elements are relevant to publishing business models, which will be subsequently discussed, resulting in a critical analysis of the well-known business models, the subscription model and the present open access model. We also propose a suite of business models separating the two main parameters for any business model in scientific publishing, which are found to be availability of research results and selection in the acquisition of information.

The subscription business model is just the model familiar from the paper age: a publisher produces a journal and charges libraries for delivery, and also for keeping toll-access digital copies posted on the web as an extra service.

A strategic alternative, which came up as a proposition for the digital documents in the digital age, is the open access business model. The policy is to post a digital document with open access on the web, independent of whether printed copies are produced and charged or not; the posting is done by either the publisher, a document provider, the university or the author's department, regardless of how the system is financed and what add-on services are being offered. Together with a chosen solution for these issues, there exist a number of different practical and experimental variations of the open access business model. One of the riddles to be elucidated in this book is why the present open access model of posting, either by a publisher as a print add-on or by a university library without many add-on services, did not result in a market penetration of more than about 15 per cent. We will show that this is because the value chain of the stakeholders is still that from the print age, and the role of each stakeholder does not tie in with its incentives. This means that the optimal business model is yet to be found: a model that will meet the requirements of researchers, give incentives to each stakeholder to allow optimal sharing and division of labour, and include the professional add-on services necessary to make use of the service.

This book is partly a compilation of existing literature and a number of previous books and papers (Roosendaal et al., 2005; Kurek et al., 2006; Zalewska-Kurek et al., 2008; Roosendaal and Geurts, 1997, 1999; Roosendaal et al., 2001a, 2001b, 2001c, 2002a, 2002b, 2003; Geurts and Roosendaal, 2001; Hummel and Roosendaal, 2001) written by the present authors on the subject of publishing business models and the strategic positioning of researchers. This volume endeavours to provide a comprehensive and integrated overview of the current knowledge, but it will not be able to provide a detailed discussion of the presented models – if this is desired, the reader is advised to consult the above-mentioned original papers.

Notes

1 This pronouncement is generally credited to Newton. Other variations are 'If I have seen further it is by standing on the shoulders of Giants' and 'If I have seen farther it is by standing on the shoulders of Giants.' The quote is from a letter by Newton to Robert Hooke of 15 February 1676 (dated 5 February 1675 using the Julian calendar with 25 March rather than 1 January as New Year's Day, equivalent to 15 February 1676 by Gregorian reckonings). A variation known from the mathematician Peter Winkler reads: 'If I have seen further it is by standing on the shoulders of Hungarians' – see http://en.wikipedia.org/wiki/Standing_on_the_shoulders_of_giants. Dwarfs standing on the shoulders of giants (Latin: *nanos gigantum humeris insidentes*) is a Western metaphor meaning 'One who develops future intellectual pursuits by understanding the research and works created by notable thinkers of the past'; this is a contemporary interpretation. However, the metaphor was first recorded in the twelfth century and attributed to Bernard of Chartres. It was famously used by the seventeenth-century scientist Isaac Newton, who wrote it as: *Pigmaei gigantum humeris impositi plusquam ipsi gigantes vident*. This pronunciation is symbolised by a picture derived from Greek mythology where the blind giant Orion carried his servant Cedalion on his shoulders.

3

Research environment

From the previous chapters it will be obvious that the overriding premise of this book is that any publishing business model should support researchers in the research process aimed at the production of knowledge. This production of knowledge itself is currently a broadly discussed topic, not only because scientific knowledge is crucial for the development of science but also because of the emerging interest of society in scientific research. Researchers therefore try to find a balance between the future roles of science and society in the production of knowledge. Production of knowledge is also at stake in the discussion on e-science, as mentioned in the Introduction.

The production of scientific knowledge requires a specific organisation (Kurek et al., 2006). This organisation creates conditions to perform scientific research. A major condition is a transparent system of sharing research results that are made public as scientific information. This organisation is made up of the research environment, consisting of researchers sharing scientific information.

In sharing information and claiming intellectual property researchers strive for recognition and reputation in their research environment (Merton, 1957; Hagstrom, 1965, 1974) as well as other rewards resulting from it, e.g. tenure (Altbach, 1996). An important aspect of scientific information, just like any information for an organisation, is that it creates competitive advantage. Recognition is part of this competitive advantage, and increases researchers' power in competing for heterogeneously distributed strategic resources. Society is more likely to share strategic assets with recognised and productive researchers, as they are considered to be more credible in delivering results. At the same time, researchers with a high reputation are able to influence and direct this society.

As stated before, scientific research is nowadays of interest not only to researchers but also to society, more specifically the societal environment, e.g. another researcher, a research institute, government or industry. The societal environment, by financing and setting the research policy and agendas, has an impact on the scientific knowledge production (Gibbons et al., 1994; Ziman, 1994). Time and effort that individual researchers have to spend on the acquisition of financial resources and adjusting to research agendas affect the production of knowledge, in the sense that their time on research is limited (Knorr-Cetina, 1981; Wilts, 2000; Laudel, 2006). Another way that the societal environment affects the production is by withholding financial support for certain ideas if they are 'too new' for external funding, don't fit research agendas or do not comply with the demand for application-driven research (Laudel, ibid.).

A relation established between researchers, as part of a research enterprise, and this research enterprise is defined as either an individual or a group of researchers performing activities contributing to scientific research, and their societal environment determines the creation of scientific knowledge in terms of choices they have to make in research, such as the choice of research goals, as well as in sharing governance in a research project (Kurek et al., 2007). Like in any relation between organisations, a main parameter determining this relation is the strategic positioning of researchers in their societal environment. Like any organisation, they position themselves in a strategic relation in order to attain their long-term goals – the overall goal of any scientific researcher is to make a contribution to scientific knowledge by doing research. To perform research activities, scientists have to make choices that lead to their strategic positioning given their specific goals. The strategic choices concern the directions of research as well as the acquisition and matching of strategic resources offered by their societal environment. The strategic position that researchers establish to attain their goals is then expressed in the relation between them and the environment.

Breaking down the societal environment

Let us expand briefly on what the environment of researchers looks like seen through their eyes and those of research institutes. With this environment we mean, as before, society at large as it influences knowledge production and is influenced by the knowledge production of the researchers. As a consequence, we do not consider at this point such things as the laboratory, lecture halls or variations in collaboration with colleagues, be this in the lab itself or outside (Knorr-Cetina, 1981; Latour, 1987). Neither do we mean the specific organisational structures of research.

The societal environment has an impact on researchers in two general ways. Firstly, on the input side the environment is research enabling; secondly, on the output side the environment absorbs the knowledge disseminated as scientific results in publications.

The foremost question for all researchers starting a research problem is whether they will be able to study the problem in such a way that they can solve it, and that this solution is suitable for the problem at hand. Apart from moral restrictions, such as mentioned in various guidelines like the UNESCO code of conduct (de Guchteneire, 2004),[1] the only condition is that it must be financed in some way or another. The trade-off between what is scientifically required to study the research problem and what society desires as outcomes results for researchers in boundary conditions to the research problems they want to study.

The following main types of conditions in research funding can be observed:

- unconditional financing
- financing with conditions on the research problem as part of a research programme
- financing with conditions on the research problem by demanding specific research objectives
- financing without conditions on the dissemination of the knowledge produced
- financing with conditions on the dissemination of the knowledge produced over time
- financing with conditions on the dissemination of the knowledge produced for specific partial results
- financing with conditions on the collaboration between researchers and their institutions.

These restrictions are institutionalised in all possible combinations in the national and international science systems around the globe. All over the world we see universities which enjoy a discretionary budget for organising research and teaching, and universities are as such an example of financing without any condition to produce knowledge (Merton, 1957). Also the prototypical institution, usually endowed by government or large, successful companies with the objective of promoting science, often enjoys unconditional financing for any researcher willing to compete for such grants, purely on the quality of its research plans. The same is true for many of the private grant donors to American universities.

It is signalled as a tendency by Gibbons et al. (1994) that instead of granting this financing for purely scientific reasons, nowadays national (and supra-national) governments are more and more using scientific research as an instrument in their policies. They do this by not only implementing research programmes but also acting as a principal contractor. In doing so, research is restricted not just to programmes but also even to specific research problems. For instance, one of the spearheads of the American Association for the Advancement of Science (AAAS) is competitiveness in science.[2] It focuses on policies concerning how public or private partnerships can be used for the advancement of competitiveness in scientific research. Next to this, there is a tendency to use formerly independent purely scientific institutions, such as the NSF (National Science Foundation, 2008) in the USA, NWO[3] (Netherlands Organisation for Scientific Research) in the Netherlands or the DFG[4] (German Research Foundation) in Germany, and many other specialised academic institutions as a vehicle in implementing such policies (see for example the triple helix discussion).

What has changed in the relation between individual research and a funding institute, like NWO, as result of the facilities offered by IT? Not more than ten years ago specific agents, having direct contact with the science institutes, disseminated and advertised the NWO funding possibilities.

The procedures were not always transparent, and often leaned towards vested interests of the universities in certain fields. As a remnant of the earlier dominant and condition-free opportunity to get grants on the basis of the quality of a proposal itself, NWO organises each year a so-called open competition in the field of legal, social and behavioural sciences. In 2008, offering the possibility of uploading proposals in digital form, this resulted within one hour in more than 500 research proposals submitted. This illustrates that the use of digital communication leads to fast and transparent procedures; it also shows that researchers still prefer to study subjects free of policy-induced science programmes. At present the system is transparent right up to the final judgement. It also includes a formal complaints procedure.[5] In its annual report for 2007 (Netherlands Organisation for Scientific Research, 2008), NWO observes a clear reduction in the number of appeals, and attributes this reduction to the improved transparency of the submission system.

In summary, the societal environment affects research by using financing schemes which vary by the type of conditions connected to the attainment of such grants.

The precise organisation of this financing varies from country to country, but the overriding principles are very similar. In society, the production of knowledge is recognised as necessary for the benefit of society at large; universities are a relevant player in society, resulting in substantial financing from society to science. This type of financing is typically without specific conditions as long as it is used directly for scientific research and academic education, and is generally allocated within research and higher education institutions.

A second substantial type of financing stems from institutions created to promote specific and targeted scientific knowledge. These institutions typically request researchers to submit specific proposals for research or ask them to compete for grants in specific subjects, programmes or fields. There is some variance in the governance that we know of at different national levels. For example, in the Netherlands these institutions are governed by the national government and its agencies. In these schemes programme conditions, i.e. conditions to the research objectives, are the rule.

We saw already that the primary goal of any researcher is sharing knowledge, and this goal is attained by making research results public, in particular to colleagues within the research community. This, however, is not a closed system. The information contained in publications is disseminated to the wider societal environment as well. This outside world wants to get scientific information in such a way that it is comprehensible and useful. Because the audience varies in its ability to comprehend the information, it is segmented. The first segment consists of fellow researchers specialised in largely the same field. This is the audience for the familiar reports of scientific research using articles and books. The second segment of the audience consists of professionals making use of scientific information but not producing such knowledge themselves in that particular field. A common example is the physician making use of the latest developments in biomedical research. The specific outlets for this segment are the so-called professional journals and books, series, handbooks, etc. In their strategic positioning it is the authors' choice to publish in these media. The third segment contains laymen or the general public. This audience is important not just to satisfy people's curiosity; it is nowadays key to getting support for research projects, as science is more and more seen as an important vehicle in the advancement of society. Transparency of the formerly closed science system is essential to find financial and other support from government and industry. Popularising science is seen in this way as more relevant than ever. More than ever the environment permeates into the science system and the science system into the environment. Anyone active in science should therefore consider his or her relation to this societal environment.

Strategic positioning of researchers

Making research results public is an important tool for researchers to position themselves in the environment. It is for this reason that we include in this chapter a brief discussion of the concept of strategic positioning, as it is relevant for establishing a strategic relation finally resulting in the production of knowledge to be made public. A more extended discussion can be found in Kurek et al. (2007), from which this description is taken.

Researchers establish such a strategic relation with the goal of creating added value. Partners decide to collaborate because in a situation in which they did not have access to resources of other researchers they would not be able to create added value and achieve their goals. Establishing this strategic relation is essentially a process of acquisition of resources, followed by negotiation between the two partners on sharing heterogeneously distributed strategic resources and governing the directions of research. Partners agree to give up governing research to a certain degree and accept sharing resources to a certain degree.

In the model of strategic positioning researchers are essentially considered as partners in the research enterprise. The activities of this enterprise include scientific activities and also organisational activities arising from and embedded in the societal environment of such an enterprise. These organisational activities determining scientific publishing and undertaken by researchers in enterprises are discussed in this section.

Researchers positioning themselves in their societal environment make a strategic choice to compete for a desired strategic position. If they decide to compete for strategic resources as offered by their societal environment, they choose to accept some degree of strategic interdependence (ibid.). They compete for these resources with researchers from both the same domain and different scientific domains in research. Scientific domains compete for being a leader in research, being recognisable and fashionable in the societal environment. This competition is about the creation of needs in the societal environment by inventing useful applications. At present, leaders are developing domains such as nanotechnology, genomics and biotechnology.[6]

The main strategic goal of scientific researchers is to contribute by research to scientific knowledge. Ziman (1994) observed that more and more researchers from all kinds of scientific domains are increasingly involved in more interdisciplinary and international research, requiring more dispersed competencies and skills as well as dispersed research facilities to deliver results. In association with this, research is nowadays becoming more capital intensive, and the organisation of research is becoming more complex. The result is that a university is often unable to finance the research independently. In this context, researchers seek other partners to share heterogeneously distributed strategic resources, such as research facilities, knowledge, etc. Next to sharing resources, they have to make a strategic choice about the extent to which they are willing to accept the partner(s) participating in governing the research project.

These choices are an integral part of the strategy leading to the strategic position of researchers, given their specific goals. Goals and choices structure their future behaviour and are therefore strategic in nature. The strategy that they develop, and therefore the strategic positioning, does not always need to be conscious and explicit. Especially, individual researchers with a primary focus on conducting research often do not reflect consciously on such strategic issues. Nonetheless, they have a long-term goal to attain, such as a career in research or academia, tenure or growth of the research enterprise, even if this is not explicit.

The strategic position that researchers establish to attain their strategic goals is expressed in relations between them and their environment, and negotiated and agreed with this environment. In this context they can be actors at different levels of aggregation: research at large, the research institute, the research group or the individual researcher. This relation is considered as an evolving process resulting in a deliberate and established collaboration. This being the case, the relation can then be seen as a (temporary) strategic alliance, joint venture, merger or even sometimes an acquisition between business partners, the business being research. To describe this relation, Kurek et al. (2007) apply a strategic management model taken from the literature on alliances, joint ventures, mergers and acquisitions by Haspeslagh and Jemison (1991). The model assumes that collaboration will be maintained if, and only if, it results in creating more added value for both partners than a situation in which such a collaboration did not exist. The model is based on two dimensions to characterise the strategic relation: organisational autonomy and strategic interdependence (ibid.).

Strategic interdependence is in this context defined as the deliberate sharing of heterogeneously distributed strategic resources, assets and capabilities between the partners in order to achieve a joint strategic goal. Strategic interdependence is a necessary but not sufficient condition for effective collaboration. This means that it is additionally assumed that close collaboration goes hand in hand with a position of high strategic interdependence, and vice versa.

Organisational autonomy of researchers is defined as self-government in deciding about research, in particular about the directions of research in a competitive environment, including setting goals, in which scientific knowledge is being created and scientific information is being used. A high degree of organisational autonomy allows actors to make autonomous decisions regarding setting goals and establishing how to attain them. A position of high strategic interdependence does not necessarily exclude a position of high organisational autonomy of researchers. A strategic position is then defined as a combination of positions in organisational autonomy and strategic interdependence.

In the model (Kurek et al., 2007), a further assumption is made that in any relation the partners each strive in principle to maximise their own organisational autonomy and minimise their strategic interdependence. However, it may not always be possible to attain the set goals. This situation may necessitate the partners giving up organisational autonomy to some acceptable degree and agreeing on strategic interdependence, also to an acceptable degree. These degrees depend on the attractiveness of the goal, such as a long-term goal like career, the growth of the group or institute, etc., and will determine what kind of collaboration is really acceptable. If a goal is very attractive and feasible the partners may compromise their mid-term goals, determining in this way an acceptable position in either organisational autonomy or strategic inter-dependence. This further means that the positions in organisational autonomy and strategic interdependence can be different for each collaboration form, i.e. having a different goal between the same partners can result in a different position.

The possible modes of strategic positioning based on these two dimensions of organisational autonomy and strategic interdependence are visualised in Figure 3.1. This model provides a continuous landscape of strategic positioning that can be roughly characterised and described by four distinct modes having different positions along the dimensions.

The first type is characterised by a position of low necessity for both organisational autonomy and strategic interdependence. In the Mode0 situation, there is virtually no relation between researchers and environment. This mode is irrelevant for the discussion on publishing business models.

A second type is a position of high necessity for organisational autonomy in combination with low necessity for strategic interdependence. In Mode1 (see Figure 3.1), researchers set research directions driven by scientific curiosity. There is a weak strategic relation between researchers and the societal environment; they do not interact with the environment as such. Therefore, they do not need to take into account societal needs and demands

Figure 3.1 Modes of strategic positioning

		Necessity for organisational autonomy (OA)	
		Low	High
Necessity for strategic interdependence (SI)	Low	Mode0	Mode1
	High	Mode2	Mode3

when setting their research goals. Moreover, they do not need to establish a relation with the environment. They are independent and autonomous in taking strategic directions in research. Because there is no strict link between researchers and societal environment, the only competition they face is within the research environment proper. Results of research are not necessarily meant to be of societal relevance; thus researchers can restrict communication and collaboration to their research environment. In this case, researchers do not need to influence this environment. This type of positioning is well known as 'ivory tower' or 'free research' (Ziman, 1994).

The third type is a position of low necessity for organisational autonomy and high necessity for strategic interdependence. In Mode2 (see Figure 3.1) the societal environment directs researchers. It influences research directions and *ipso facto* influences the scientific products they deliver. This means that researchers match their own research problems to existing research programmes based on the demand of the societal environment. According to Novotny et al. (2003) they are 'context-sensitive'. Examples of this mode are consultancy and research outsourced by a financial partner when this partner demands particular studies to be carried out and the researchers comply. In this case they do not influence their societal environment in creating demand for their scientific products, but supply in reaction to the demand of the societal environment. The researcher listens to the environment and fulfils societal needs. By societal need we mean a need which is explicitly expressed by the partner of the researcher, as a representative of the societal environment, in the strategic relation. The properties of this mode show that it is comparable with Gibbons et al.'s (1994) Mode2, or strategic research as broadly described by them, and Ziman (1994).

The Mode3 position of high necessity for both organisational autonomy and strategic interdependence means that researchers share resources with the environment, like Mode2 researchers. However, contrary to Mode2 researchers, research entrepreneurs have the opportunity to be autonomous in determining the directions of research. They retain their own responsibilities for directing a project. Research entrepreneurs are seen as an answer to the need for a social contract rewarding all parties, as proposed by Gibbons (1999): research entrepreneurs interact with the societal environment in such a way that 'they speak to the environment and the environment speaks back to them'. The two parties, researchers and societal environment, are keen on establishing this strategic relation: researchers because their work will be funded, and the societal environment because scientific results will be applied. Research entrepreneurs, like business entrepreneurs, influence the societal environment by creating demand for their scientific products. Being a part of this societal environment, they can recognise and define a societal need for improving and further developing new or existing products, and deliver such products.

Research entrepreneurs, instead of being just oriented towards society, are fully intertwined with the societal environment and strategically interdependent with this environment. At the same time, as stated above, research entrepreneurs are highly autonomous. This position of high autonomy is expressed in decisions regarding research goals to meet, with whom to collaborate or who could and should be the potential users of the research results. Research entrepreneurs increase in this way their ability to influence this environment.

Summarising, a continuum of modes describes the strategic positioning, with four ideal types as pivotal points.

As noted before, the fact that there is a continuum means also that one and the same actor can display a combination of different positions in different relations compatible with the set long-term goals. This is important to consider in applications, in particular in relation to publishing.

Scientific information, and therefore any business model for scientific publishing, is intended to serve researchers in research, and thus in their strategic positioning in the environment, in particular in claiming the intellectual property of an invention. And this can only be achieved by making research results public to all researchers concerned, as collaborators and as competitors.

Competition in research

As we have seen, one aspect of scientific information, like information in any business organisation, is to create competitive advantage for the research enterprise. Competitive advantage based on scientific information not only enhances the influence of researchers in their research environment but also leads to a better strategic position in the societal environment. For this reason, we will deal in a succinct way with this aspect of competition, in particular how it relates to making research results public and acquiring scientific information. A more extensive description can be found in Zalewska-Kurek et al. (2008).

Competition in the research environment is a well-known feature and has been studied extensively. One of the first contributors to this subject was Merton (1957), stating that the increasing number of researchers and the popularity of particular scientific domains cause clustering of research areas into a limited group, and may lead to multiple discoveries. He illustrates his argument by the quest for priority of discovery, with examples of conflicts over priority between Newton and Hook, and Newton and Leibniz. Since Merton, many other studies have significantly contributed to this subject (Gaston, 1970, 1973, 1978; Hagstrom, 1965, 1974; Collins, 1968; McCain, 1991). Hagstrom (1965, 1974) confirmed Merton's discovery of competition in research. According to his study in physics and biology, over 60 per cent of his respondents were faced at least once with the fact that somebody else published a solution for a research problem they were working on.

Other results delivered by researchers from 14 countries in 1992–1993 also confirm the influence of competition in the research environment. These results show the importance of publishing research results for competitive purposes, in particular for tenure. Researchers from Israel (81 per cent), Germany (78 per cent), Sweden (58 per cent), Australia (64 per cent) and the USA (75 per cent) agreed that 'it is difficult for persons to achieve tenure if they do not publish' (Altbach, 1996).

Gaining competitive advantage will also result in a number of rewards. Firstly, research results made public as scientific information, if accepted by the research environment, contribute to scientific knowledge. Secondly, the research environment offers recognised researchers rewards like scientific position, tenure, research projects, requests to review scientific papers and grant proposals, membership of an editorial board or programme committees of international conferences, invited talks at the international level, visiting fellowships (Laudel, 2006) and consultancy opportunities in both research and the societal environment. Recognition and reputation help researchers to acquire strategic resources from the societal environment, as argued before.

In this competition, scientific information has been seen to play a major role. Although, as discussed above, from the researcher's point of view scientific information should be common property and should in principle be shared, this is not always done for competitive reasons. Campbell et al. (2000) indicate that some researchers in academic medicine withhold data from their younger colleagues who do not have an established reputation, as well as from researchers commercialising their knowledge or publishing, in their opinion, too many papers. Other research conducted by Ceci (1998) reports on secretive behaviour among university researchers who do not share data before claiming intellectual property by publishing or patenting. Researchers are not willing to share their results before claiming property rights, as they are afraid of plagiarism or commercial abuse (Barnes, 1987; Campbell et al., 2000). Needless to say, sharing scientific information is important for the development of scientific knowledge and minimising duplication of each other's research (Campbell and Blumenthal, 2002).

Roosendaal and Geurts (1999) and later Campbell and Blumenthal (2002) state that exchange of information is essential for the integrity of science. Research is only valid if it can be repeated, and published results are only valid if reproducible and not falsified by other researchers. Applied research methods should be transparent for the research environment. This means that others may request materials and data used in particular research. Withholding data precludes quality control. Campbell et al. (2000) discover in their research on geneticists that secrecy and withholding data preclude confirming published research.

Secrecy, however, might be concomitant with research funded by the societal environment, e.g. by industry (Wadman, 1996). This leads to specific conditions on organisational autonomy. Such conditions, as seen before, are often required by industry – that information produced in joint research is kept confidential or its publication is delayed.

Next to having an impact on making research results public, competition also has an impact on the acquisition of scientific information. Researchers must 'monitor and anticipate what competitors... intend' (Yoxen, 1988). This is an aspect of selection by the researcher in following closely most recent publications in the same scientific domain to avoid multiple discoveries. In acquiring scientific information, researchers use the names of their competitors and collaborators as search tools.

Summarising, competition is a driver for scientific publishing. Competition drives researchers to create new research results, trigger innovative changes and make their results public.

Notes

1 See also the ongoing activities on this subject at http://portal.unesco.org/shs/en/ev.php-URL_ID=1837& URL_DO=DO_TOPIC&URL_SECTION=201.html.
2 See the AAAS website, www.aaas.org.
3 See the NWO website, www.nwo.nl/nwohome.nsf/pages/ SPPD_5R2QE7_Eng, especially the subsidies pages.
4 See the DFG website, www.dfg.de/en/index.html, especially the research funding pages.
5 Details are available on the NWO website at www.nwo.nl/ nwohome.nsf/pages/NWOA_75MC65_Eng.
6 These scientific domains are strongly financially supported by, for example, the European Union Framework Programmes.

Acquisition of scientific information

That business models for scientific publishing should serve researchers in the acquisition of scientific information also means that these models should take into account that such acquisition is considerably determined by the strategic positioning of researchers and the competition they are facing.

Scientific information has to be relevant, available, up to date and retrievable. It is recognised in the study of Tenopir and King (2000) that researchers spend among other activities on average 100–150 hours per year (depending on the scientific domain) on acquiring the information required for their research. This is a sizeable fraction (5–10 per cent) of the working year. Moreover, research is always done under some time pressure; there is a deadline for a conference paper, a presentation or a report for the societal environment, etc. Researchers want to acquire scientific information effectively and efficiently. They thus require professional services that will optimise their acquisition effort.

The way in which competition in the research environment determines the acquisition of scientific information is twofold. A lack of relevant and available scientific information that has to be acquired and scrutinised by researchers can lead to a crisis, or some discontinuity in research. This crisis situation can further result in reduced strategic positioning in the environment, and finally in loss of reputation or the opportunity to acquire strategic resources. Scientific information is therefore a requisite for gaining and retaining competitive advantage.

Second, competition determines the manner in which researchers acquire scientific information. Next to usual daily acquisition, such as browsing the internet and scientific journals, journal tables of contents alerts, abstracting and indexing services, references in other articles, scientific communication with collaborators, etc. (Brown, 1999; Tenopir and King, 2000; Davis, 2004), researchers acquire information by searching what their competitors have discovered recently. This is an aspect of selection by researchers in their attempts to follow publications in the same scientific domain to avoid multiple discoveries.

The efficiency of the acquisition of scientific information can be improved by enhancing the power of selection by researchers. This can be done by providing pre-selection services, e.g. specific services to disclose information effectively and efficiently. Researchers do thus require 'basic' services making certified, i.e. peer-reviewed, scientific information generally available. These basic services include selection tools naturally based on the structure of scientific information.

Peer review is essential for the research environment and therefore core to any business model for scientific publishing. By 'branding' their contribution, peer review serves researchers striving for recognition in the research environment. Peer review also serves researchers, especially junior scientists and students, in selecting information, as they are able to choose between different brands. Especially in a case when researchers as readers are not in the same learned field as the author, they may be extremely dependent on pre-selection by peer reviewing. In this way, peer review supports the power of selection by researchers and is important for the acquisition of scientific information.

Peer review serves the reputation of researchers. Researchers competing for recognition do not want to publish in low-quality journals and hardly want to refer to such journals. Such journals may lose their audience and revenue stream (Prosser, 2005). Therefore, peer review should be a basic service included in any business model for scientific publishing.

There may be a temptation to weaken the review scrutiny in the open access model, if and because researchers pay for their publications. Also, the university acting as publisher should not manage the certification of research results of its own employees (Roosendaal, 2004).

As Hilf and Wätjen (2001) and Prosser (2005) pointed out, open access to digital documents allows in principle a much wider variety of peer-review types. Different types include peer review before or after posting on the web, pre-evaluation by a community of an open access posted preprint, voluntary reviewing, with the result that the referee is not obliged to act and is not under time pressure, and peer review of a document already posted as a preprint and not withdrawn if not accepted for publication. The *Directory of Open Access Journals*, an international registry of open access journals, shows an impressive list of peer-reviewed journals.[1]

The new, richer and more specific types of peer review (Hilf and Wätjen, 2001) possible for digital open access journals give new hope not only to professionalising further peer review as such but also to counteracting eventual abuse of peer reviewing as experienced in the paper age.[2] Publishers have to rely on the competence and expertise of their chosen chief editor and editors for the professional standards of a journal. Thus, in a case of misjudgement in selecting the chief editor, a low-quality journal may live for quite a while undetected.[3]

Analysis of the strategic positioning of a research institute

As an example of the strategic positioning of researchers we use research performed by staff of the MESA+ Institute for Nanotechnology at the University of Twente in the Netherlands (Zalewska-Kurek, 2008). The expertise of researchers at MESA+[4] concentrates primarily on bio-nanotechnology, nano-structured materials, nano-electronics, micro- and nano-fluidics, photonics and societal, ethical and philosophical aspects of nanosciences and technology. The institute employs 237 FTEs in research, plus a large number of support staff including cleanroom and laboratory technicians.

MESA+ collaborates with a number of key players in the field of nanotechnology, including IMAC in Belgium, iNano in Denmark, the IRC in the UK, Forschungszentrum Jülich and Forschungszentrum Karlsruhe in Germany and many others. Apart from collaborating with researchers, the institute has established relations with its societal environment, more specifically with its representatives, such as the European Union at the international level, and at the national level the NWO, various ministries and industry.

Strategic relations with these actors can be analysed using the model of strategic positioning presented in the previous chapter. But what exactly does it mean be positioned in Mode0, 1, 2 or 3, in particular with respect to the acquisition of scientific information and making research results public? With the example of MESA+ we translate the model of strategic positioning presented in Chapter 3 to study the behaviour of individual researchers.

We present here the results of in-depth personal interviews with researchers. The sample is stratified along all scientific ranks: from PhD students, post-docs and assistant and associate professors to full professors. All the researchers are involved in research. Some conduct research full time, like PhD students and post-docs; some spend a considerable part of their time on teaching and supervising students, like assistant and associate professors. Usually assistant and associate professors are involved, next to management and the organisation of research, in strategic management, though not to the same extent as full professors. This means that they acquire research funds from their societal environment – this usually takes time that could otherwise be spent on research.

The researchers were interviewed about their behaviour when making their research results public and when acquiring scientific information. The interview results were coded in terms of the two dimensions of strategic interdependence and organisational autonomy, so as to be able to observe modes of strategic positioning. The example of MESA+ shows relations between the interviewed researchers and colleagues with whom they work and publish; the presented positions of the interviewed researchers are averaged over a number of studied relations of these researchers. The results of the study conducted at MESA+ show that the interviewed researchers are mostly positioned in Mode3, as research entrepreneurs (shown in Figure 4.1). This means that they are both highly autonomous and highly interdependent.

In terms of making research results public and acquiring scientific information, these researchers do not always write

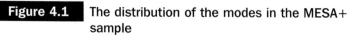

Figure 4.1 The distribution of the modes in the MESA+ sample

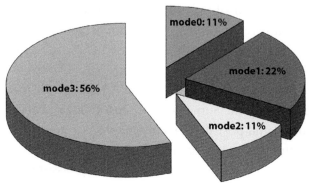

articles themselves (first drafts); rather, they limit their input to rewriting or editing what their co-authors wrote. They are often involved in discussions on outlines of articles and on final drafts. They are thus highly dependent on researchers they publish with – usually the scientific staff of their research groups or collaborative groups. High dependence is also indicated by the extent to which a researcher relies on his colleagues in acquiring scientific information. Research entrepreneurs rely on information they receive from colleagues. This means that they use other researchers as a source of scientific information, for example by asking colleagues about new developments in the particular domain. Highly interdependent researchers also acquire scientific information from colleagues in their domain, by either contacting them directly or meeting them at conferences.

Some researchers are not directly involved in the writing process, but provide facilities and acquire financial resources for research. Their input is then connected with the research process, specifically in the organisation and management of the process, but not with publishing results of the research itself. They are highly dependent on their co-authors in writing.

Research entrepreneurs are also highly autonomous. This means that they make decisions on what, where and when to make results public. They decide what should be included in an article, e.g. what should be the line of reasoning, what references should be included, etc. They judge when the quality of work is of a sufficient level to be scrutinised by external reviewers. They also decide to which journal an article should be submitted. In terms of the acquisition of scientific information, research entrepreneurs are not being influenced by others in what they should acquire and when; rather, they influence the behaviour of others.

Next to Mode3, we see that a sizeable group of researchers position themselves in Mode1. Mode1 researchers do not depend on their colleagues when making research results public and acquiring scientific information. It does not necessarily mean that they work completely in isolation and do not ask for advice, etc., but that other researchers do not have a direct influence on their decisions. The interviewed researchers are rarely positioned in an extreme or pure Mode1 position. They share some of the decisions with their colleagues, with whom they publish their research results. In principle, Mode1 researchers do not depend on their colleagues in making research results public. They write and edit their articles themselves and make autonomous decisions on what should be included, when articles can be submitted and to which journals they should be sent. Also, when acquiring scientific information they remain autonomous and independent. They do not rely on their colleagues as much as research entrepreneurs, meaning that they generally acquire information from the internet, databases, scientific journals, etc. Similar to the research entrepreneur, they influence others' behaviour and are not being influenced to a large extent, for example when checking if somebody else has already claimed intellectual property rights for similar ideas or developments. Both

Mode3 and Mode1 researchers personally select this kind of information.

Our next prototype is Mode2. Mode2 researchers are highly dependent on their colleagues, just like research entrepreneurs, but unlike entrepreneurs they are less autonomous. These researchers usually comment on drafts that other researchers wrote. They are not the main stakeholders in the writing process. They do not make autonomous decisions on what, when and where work should be published; they either make such decisions jointly with other co-authors, or others make them. An example is a researcher contributing to research of others, adding expertise to a paper without being responsible for the entire paper or deciding to which journal it should be submitted. At MESA+ an example could be technicians participating to a certain extent in research. These technicians delivering on the demand of researchers are highly dependent on the researchers and less autonomous (even though they might suggest solutions, they are supposed to comply with set research goals). Mode2 researchers depend on their colleagues when acquiring scientific information and at the same time they are influenced by them, e.g. by students asking for specific information that has to be acquired.

Mode0 researchers do not establish strategic relations with their colleagues when making their research results public. This does not mean that there is no relation at all; in practice, as observed at MESA+, Mode0 researchers are very close to Mode2 – they publish together with their colleagues, but the input of these colleagues is not always sufficient to conclude that the interdependence is high. These researchers are less autonomous. Although they have influence on the content of their articles, they do not make decisions on journals to which their articles should be sent. Their superiors often make these decisions.

Motives to publish

The main motives to publish emerging from this research are presented in Figure 4.2. The interviewed researchers publish results of their research for any one or a combination of three reasons: striving for recognition, sharing knowledge and external pressure. External pressure means that, because of being a member of a group or as a researcher in general, they are expected to publish, or to show that public money is spent well, etc. The motive of sharing knowledge is perceived by some of the respondents as a sort of 'idealistic' reason; some even said 'idealistic' verbatim. It was often a first answer given to this question, followed by external pressure or recognition. From these reactions we conclude that the motive of sharing knowledge is a sort of cliché. A sizeable proportion of the sample (43 per cent) publish because they want to share knowledge and gain recognition in their scientific domain, and because of the external pressure mentioned above. Twenty-five per cent of the interviewed researchers publish because they want to be recognised as authors of their discoveries, want to share knowledge and/or are under some sort of pressure.

Figure 4.2   The distribution of motives to publish

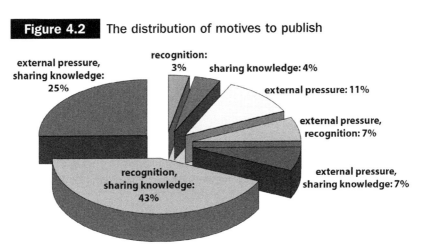

Choice of a journal

When developing business models it is important to be aware of drivers to submit articles to certain scientific journals. The interviewed researchers, when choosing journals for submission, consider which journal is most prestigious and which has the highest impact factor (that in consequence brings them recognition) considering the quality of the article and the scope of the journal. They also consider the audience for their article. Is the paper addressed to a broad or a specific audience? Next to these motives, they often check if they or their co-authors know editors of journals. They sometimes submit articles to journals of which they are editors. They might be invited to write a paper. All these aspects are perceived by the interviewed researchers as giving a sort of 'easiness' in submitting articles. As seen in Figure 4.3, the majority of the interviewed researchers are driven by recognition and audience when choosing a journal for the submission of papers.

Figure 4.3 The distribution of motives for choosing journals when submitting articles

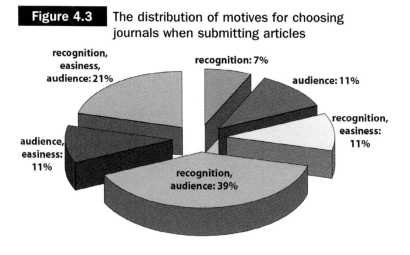

Institutional strategic positioning and production of knowledge

The model of strategic positioning presented in this book illustrates that the strategic positioning of researchers affects the production of knowledge. If the value proposition in a research business model is to increase the production of knowledge, it is advisable to look carefully at the strategic positioning of the researchers involved in the research organisation for which the business model is being developed.

The results of the interviews with the researchers at MESA+ show that the degrees of strategic interdependence (SI) and organisational autonomy (OA) of researchers influence the number of articles produced per year. Figure 4.4 indicates the number of articles that the researchers in the MESA+ sample would produce assuming specific combinations of SI and OA. This number ranges from no articles to over 100 articles in the extreme cases of strategic interdependence and organisational autonomy both being close to 1.

The production of knowledge is seen to increase with organisational autonomy and strategic interdependence. Mode2 is seen to be slightly more productive than Mode1. The most productive mode is seen to be Mode3 – the research entrepreneur. This means that those researchers who are dependent on their colleagues and are, at the same time, autonomous in making decisions on the content of a publication, if the quality of research results is sufficient to be submitted and where to publish are most productive.

| Figure 4.4 | Predicted production of knowledge in terms of papers produced per year for the MESA+ sample as a function of strategic interdependence and organisational autonomy |

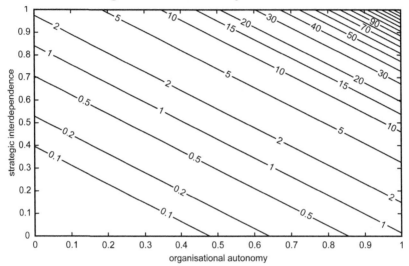

Scientific information in a broader perspective

Up to this point we have restricted the discussion to scientific information for research. However, scientific information is not only applied in research, but plays an important role in education. Developments in scientific information thus have consequences for the R&HE institute as a whole, and affect in particular its competitive position. In this vein, we will now make a brief excursion into these arenas before going back to discussing scientific information with a primary focus on research. It will be evident that the developments in research discussed in the previous chapters also have consequences for the educational tasks of R&HE institutes. This is in particular an issue for those courses that are tightly connected to the research areas of a university, such as masters' and PhD courses: curricula need to be tailored towards the specific modes of research. Curricula are seen to become generally more concise and at the same time more focused, in particular under the influence of the bachelor-master system. The result of these changes is that people will be less educated in the 'academic' way, but more trained to apply their knowledge directly in the short term. As a result, the demand for 'academic' education and continuous professional development becomes stronger. Universities will have to compete with other institutions offering academic professional education, with the goal of adding to their revenue streams.

These developments have resulted over the past years, and still result, in changes in the management of universities and research institutes, such as development into an entrepreneurial university (Clark, 2001) and the creation of consortia transforming into transnational or even global networks of centres of excellence in a highly competitive world.

Scientific information is thus part of wider institutional knowledge management for research and teaching, as well as the overall competitive position of the R&HE institute.

Education

Developments in scientific information affect not only the way we do research, but the way we do education as well. Information technology has introduced new applications of communication in education through a multitude of combinations of synchronous and asynchronous interaction, and the end of this development is not yet in sight.

The following aspects relating to scientific information are particularly important in education (Roosendaal et al., 2005):

- *connectivity*, relating to the possibility of establishing interactions between students, instructors and groups of both

- *content*, relating to the use and specifically the reuse of content from a wide, disparate variety of sources, such as the web, but also including traditional archives

- *culture*, relating to the cultural and educational aspects of the interaction between instructors and students, students and students, instructors and instructors – online and more traditionally face to face.

Demands for educational content result in demands for information that will widely overlap with research and education requirements for scientific information, not least for advanced, i.e. masters' and PhD, students. Education will at least in part draw on the same sources and resources while making use of the same technical infrastructure. For this reason, it is relevant to analyse jointly the organisational and in particular the business issues related to education and research information, as these may well influence business models in scientific information.

In education, a universal engine for change is the desire of students to choose their own teachers and of teachers to select their students.[5] These desires lead to demand-driven education with high student mobility. This development bears some analogy with the discussion on the strategic position of researchers presented in the previous chapter. Here we could analyse students in a similar way in terms of modes, resulting in the same landscape characterised by the same four distinct modes. This means that in education we see a definite development towards the 'student entrepreneur' and the 'teacher entrepreneur', both having a high necessity for autonomy and strategic interdependence with respect to each other. This new strategic positioning is furthered by high mobility of students, albeit a virtual mobility enabled by IT, and is reflected in greater segmentation of student and teacher needs. This mobility is expected to show up particularly for masters' students, and has led to the introduction of international masters. The introduction of the bachelor/master structure[6] at European institutions is intended to further the mobility of students and will spur the development of web-based and blended learning where students are more mobile and will hop virtually from one institution to another – becoming real 'student entrepreneurs'.

This new strategic positioning of students will as a consequence mean that academic teaching at institutions will develop from a local supply-oriented service to an international demand-oriented service. This will result in more intense competition between institutions and hence a higher quality demand.

These developments will lead to a change in the relation between the teacher and the student: from rather static supply and demand to a competitive adjustment to actual demand, or in other words a 'student entrepreneur' and a 'teacher entrepreneur'. From the point of view of the student this means a more individual conceptualisation of teaching: a new apprenticeship model between teacher and student viewing the student as a young, individual and continuously developing scientist, thus increasing the student's autonomy, and a more interactive teaching concept, increasing the strategic interdependence and leading to a new competitive orientation on actual demand.

Institutional considerations

Following the above, for the development of scientific information it is relevant (Roosendaal et al., 2005; Roosendaal, 2004) to take into account that investments in information systems will be stimulated by educational purposes as well as demands for research information. Such information systems will include course management systems and course material. It is very possible that this will lead at many universities to the development of integrated study and information environments requiring document servers, browsers and archives. Important in this respect is the fact that these facilities will have to meet the same technical requirements as are needed for scientific information. In short, the universities will develop for educational purposes a publishing and archiving facility equivalent to that needed for scientific information. The only difference is that the archiving facility is probably more focused on the short- to medium-term archiving required for education, rather than on long-term archiving as required for scientific information.

If this development becomes widespread, and there is every reason to assume this, it will lead to alignment consequences for stakeholders, both internal within the institute and external. Internal alignment is needed between research, education and scientific information, mostly represented by the library as a separate body within the institution, while external alignment is needed between the institute and the other R&HE institutes with their institutions, independent libraries such as national libraries, publishers and other intermediaries. This alignment poses a further challenge to the business models under consideration.

Notes

1 By January 2009 the *Directory of Open Access Journals* listed 3,812 peer-reviewed open access journals; see www.doaj.org.

2 Discussed at the International Union of Pure and Applied Physics Workshop on Scientific Misconduct and the Role of Physics Journals in its Investigation and Prevention, London, 13–14 October 2003 – see www.iupap.org/wg/ communications/ethics/index.html. For a summary see www. isn-oldenburg.de/~hilf/vortraege/london03/ report2EPS.pdf.

3 Recently it became known that a man called N. El Naschie ran a peer-reviewed journal for a major publisher for a long time undetected, using random machine-created articles – see www.zeit.de/2009/03/N-El-Naschie.

4 See the website of the MESA+ Institute for Nanotechnology, University of Twente, at www.mesaplus.utwente.nl.

5 See the Bologna Declaration of 19 June 1999: Joint Declaration of the European Ministers of Education, at www.bologna-berlin2003.de/pdf/bologna_declaration.pdf.

6 Ibid.

5

The market for scientific information

In the previous chapters we have analysed the environment in which researchers work, which was seen to comprise the research environment proper and the wider societal environment. We analysed the strategic positions researchers can choose in doing research, the consequences this has for the competitive conditions to which researchers are subjected and what this means for researchers when making results public and acquiring scientific information. All these elements are relevant ingredients for the market for scientific information that we are now ready to analyse in more detail.

On the basis of the analyses in Chapters 3 and 4 we can define the market for scientific information as consisting of researchers, teachers and students in research and higher education institutions worldwide, be these public or private. The products in this market comprise scientific information, i.e. research results and data, as texts, audio, video, etc., and all other management and administrative information required for scientific research and academic teaching.

As we noted in the vision described in the Introduction, research and academic teaching demand comprehensive availability of scientific information. This demand has been virtually constant over centuries, and we do not expect it to alter. The demand is a permanent driver for change in the management concepts required for scientific information, given new external conditions such as developments in technology, and defines the desired and required value chain. This demand leads to a continuous recreation of the market for scientific information. The market is always looking for synergies and opportunities leading to further integration of all information in research and education. This results in a continuous evolution, and the technical, content and organisational consequences for the exchange of information in research and education need be continually considered.

Developments in the scientific information market

It is well beyond the scope of this work to describe the full history of the scientific information market. Other books are much more suited to such a description (Meadows, 1998; Frederiksson, 2001; Schöpfel, 2008). In this book we will restrict our review to some pertinent developments relevant to our strategy discussion.

The scientific information market has developed over a period of more than 300 years, characterised by a steady growth of information (de Solla Price, 1986). A recent development for this market is the internet, as this promises, as discussed in the previous chapters, new options for sharing information that are more commensurate to the scientific habitus. Over the past ten years this internet development has resulted in considerable changes in the scientific information world, in particular how information is being used and integrated in the research and teaching processes. It is for this reason that over the past years universities and their libraries, publishers and other intermediaries have invested in technological innovation in this area.

The consequence is that with the internet, publishing has become more capital intensive. Combined with the enormous possibilities to automate and rationalise the technical part of the publication process that scales with size, this has led to further clustering of publishers resulting in ever fewer companies, with each of the remaining operators controlling an expanding market share of published papers. The concentration of publishers has strengthened their strategic and negotiating positions *vis-à-vis* the scientific world, i.e. the universities and research institutes. This development was not expected at the outset of the internet; rather, the internet was expected to empower researchers, and in this way the scientific community, and even to weaken the strategic position of the publisher.

What kind of strategies can universities develop and implement to their benefit? Only if science can build a strong position and be a strong partner in the business model will it be possible to create a more transparent market, based on comprehensive information for all stakeholders. Universities have been integrating scientific information in in-house systems to make the scientific process more effective and efficient. The development of repositories provides universities with the opportunity to strengthen their joint position in the value chain versus other stakeholders, in particular the publishers. Indeed, these repositories allow universities to make information widely available; it feels as if scientific information is coming back home to the *alma mater*. The number and size of the university institutional repositories providing open access to the documents of their scientists are ever increasing, albeit slowly,[1] as the Registry of Open Access Repositories (ROAR)[2] shows.

Similarly, as with publishers, we have seen a concentration in the scientific community landscape – not so much in terms of real mergers, but in buyer concentration in consortia of universities and research institutes, in this way strengthening their position *vis-à-vis* the publishers. Another mode of concentration is seen in consortia of universities and research institutes aiming to develop networks on a national basis, such as in the Netherlands, the UK, the USA, Germany and many other countries.

A major strategic initiative is the open access development, culminating in the Berlin Declaration on Open Access to Knowledge in the Sciences and Humanities[3] postulating general access to scientific information. EPrints is serving the ROAR registry of institutional self-archiving policy commitments, with their various concepts regarding mandating whether or not authors post their documents in different ways. Many universities in many countries have welcomed and signed this declaration and are active in finding ways to adhere to it. This has resulted in an abundance of initiatives and strategies. A European Union committee worked out a detailed recommendation,[4] which stimulated a Europe-wide petition to the EU to propose a weak form of mandate. Some universities adopted the strategy of setting positive incentives for their local authors and faculties to post their new scientific documents on the university's open access repository, most successfully and prominently the University of Minho, Portugal, which offered every faculty extra funding as soon as it reached 100 per cent open access of its documents on the university IR.[5] The first university to mandate open access successfully was the University of Southampton;[6] this was pushed through by a prominent early promoter of open access, Stevan Harnad.[7]

E-science thus creates a new strategic element leading to even more changes to the value chain of scientific information. As we have seen, e-science means essentially the sharing of scientific information in a comprehensive network of R&HE institutions. It means a further step towards the goal of full availability of scientific results, including primary results and other pertinent data, and thus a further step towards full integration of information into the research process. This development is probably even more important for smaller and medium-sized institutions: it is a *conditio sine qua non* for them if they want to participate fully in research, as it is nowadays organised in a more and more programmatic approach in a national or international setting. Only when firmly embedded in e-science will these institutions be able to participate effectively and efficiently in projects of that scale. E-science means sharing of information at all levels in the research process, both informal and formal. In Germany, the government has put up a support programme to foster e-science and grid-computing.[8]

Growth of scientific information and its consequences

On a worldwide scale, scientific information has been and is still growing at about 5 per cent or more on an annual basis in terms of articles or units of work published. It has been growing at roughly this rate for a period of several centuries. Such growth is well known as exponential, and results in a doubling of the worldwide annual scientific output every ten to 15 years. This has primarily been the result of a growth in the number of researchers worldwide; on balance, the productivity per researcher has not changed much (de Solla Price, 1986). Scarceness of available human resources will exhaust this growth in a natural way. Growth in scientific output can thus result only from an increase in efficacy and efficiency in the research process. This depends on the efficacy and efficiency of sharing information, i.e. of the scientific information system.

This growth of scientific information has given rise to a debate on 'information overload', suggesting exorbitant growth of information. As we have seen, this 'overload' is the result of the steady growth of scientific research output, as witnessed already for centuries and as needed to sustain scientific progress. Growth slower than exponential will lead to diminishing returns, hampering the rate of scientific progress. Despite this fact, some stakeholders, in particular from the library world, have advocated reducing the growth of information. This may solve problems for archives, and especially libraries, but research evidently is not interested and should not be interested in a solution to the 'information overload' that will hamper scientific progress by reducing the availability of information. Rather, research wants to find ways to deal more effectively and efficiently with this ever-growing pile of information.

We can thus safely assume that the volume of available information will continue to grow, and possibly even at a higher rate, as enormous amounts of primary data will be an ever-increasing part of it. As a consequence, the overall costs of availability, i.e. the costs for storing the information in such a way as to make it widely available, will continue to grow in some sort of commensurate way, depending on the technology being used. This rather autonomous growth of scientific information resulted in the past in more and more journals to cover the expansion in research areas, and existing journals have grown in volume. In this way, the overall system will become more expensive if we want all this burgeoning information to be widely available for researchers. An alternative is to develop innovative business models providing full availability of scientific information, as required for sharing this information when made public, while at the same time reducing the costs for acquiring the information. This means that one has to find a new, balanced value chain, and consequently a new division of labour between the stakeholders commensurate with their inherent incentives and the new technical possibilities.

The market and its forces

The market for scientific information and its forces are defined as conditions that have to be fulfilled by the environment, allowing researchers to position themselves in this environment.

It has been stated before (Roosendaal and de Ruiter, 1990; Geurts and Roosendaal, 2001; Roosendaal et al., 2005; Roosendaal et al., 2008) that the driving force for this market is that 'authors want to publish *more*' and have their product widely available, while 'readers want to read *less*', but want to be informed of all that is relevant for their research at hand. Readers want this information available just in time. They want to be guaranteed that they can and will be informed of all that is relevant to them.

The market for scientific information thus consists of researchers as producers of knowledge (authors) and as users (such as readers) of knowledge. As argued in the previous chapters, it is the overall goal of researchers to produce knowledge. And in the process of production of knowledge they acquire and make use of scientific information produced by others. Therefore, when we talk about the market we talk about the combination of the production of knowledge and the acquisition of scientific information.

Next to these generic stakeholders (researchers) and other stakeholders such as libraries, digital networks, publishers, agents, etc., the market consists of the product of scientific information, as the objective of researchers is to share scientific information. As we know, researchers are not only producers but also heavy users of scientific information produced by others. This is a very important premise that has to be made explicit, implying that scientific knowledge, if not shared, does not exist. What is happening in the mind of the researcher if not made explicit cannot be measured or observed: it does not exist. Scientific knowledge can only be observed if we define under what conditions such an observation can be made. The condition here is that scientific information must have been made public.

Forces that can be observed in this market are therefore related to researchers and scientific information itself. The driving force for researchers in producing scientific knowledge is recognition. As stated in Chapter 4, important motives to publish research results are recognition and visibility. Another motive given by researchers – publishing in order to acquire funds for research (external pressure) – is interrelated to recognition.

As we have seen earlier, recognition leads to reputation, and researchers report produced knowledge as an instrument in the acquisition of resources. Reputation increases their chances in acquiring resources. Competition has been seen not to be a goal in itself for researchers. The goal is to be recognised, and competition is the organisation of actions and efforts of researchers to attain this goal. One of the strategic choices researchers make is to collaborate with other researchers. This should be seen as a specific competitive strategy. In fact, it is a sort prisoner's dilemma, in the sense that it constitutes a simple calculation of profits, costs and losses. Before starting to collaborate, researchers consider with whom to work, under which conditions, what can be gained from working with others, what is lost in the case that the project fails, and the risks in setting up a particular collaboration.

Recognition and competition are attributes of the generic stakeholders, while availability and selection are attributes of the product. Researchers in the market for scientific information require knowledge that can be easily acquired. It has to be available and easy to select. Only in this way can researchers gain a competitive advantage in competing with others. The forces are complementary, and should be properly balanced with regards to the researchers and their positioning in the environment.

Following these arguments, the driving forces in the scientific information market are *recognition, competition, availability* and *selection*. These forces can be shown in a tetrahedron (Figure 5.1) representing the following equation:

Scientific information market =
f(recognition, competition, availability, selection)

Figure 5.1   **Tetrahedron representing the market forces in scientific information**

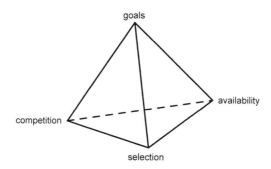

Functions in scientific information

Following Roosendaal and Geurts (1997) and Roosendaal and de Ruiter (1990), the main functions of scientific information can be defined as *registration, awareness, certification* and *archiving*. We can visualise these four main functions in another tetrahedron, as shown in Figure 5.2.

This tetrahedron represents the following equation:

Scientific information =
        f(registration, archiving, awareness, certification)

stating that scientific information is assumed to be comprehensively described in terms of these four main functions.

As scientific information only exists if claimed by the author by the act of registration, and as it is only useful if it can be retrieved, we need only deal with that part of the tetrahedron containing the registration and archiving functions. This tetrahedron will thus collapse to the representation presented in Figure 5.3.

We can now observe two axes: the vertical axis describes registration and awareness, which can both be seen as different aspects of scientific observation, whereas the

Figure 5.2 **Tetrahedron representing the functions in scientific information**

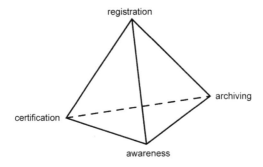

Figure 5.3 Functions in scientific information

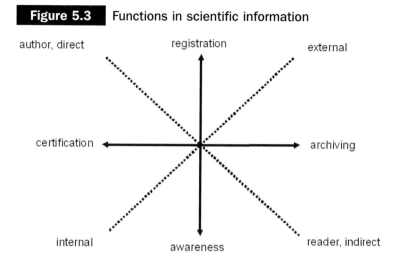

horizontal axis describes certification and archiving, which in turn can be seen as different aspects of scientific judgement.

Inspecting Figure 5.3, we find that there are information functions that are *internal* to the research and education process and information functions that are *external* to this process. As internal functions can in principle not be outsourced, from a strategic point of view only the functions external to the research and education process, registration and archiving, can be outsourced, but only under well-considered conditions to external stakeholders, e.g. to a publisher or repository, a library or another intermediary in the process.

Figure 5.3 constitutes a representation of the overall scientific information process as part of the research and education process.

As an illustration of the four information functions, let us briefly analyse (Roosendaal et al., 2001a) the birth of the first research journals, *Le Journal des Sçavans* (Paris) and the *Philosophical Transactions* of the Royal Society of

London. The main reason for the birth of these journals was the growth of research activity in the seventeenth century and the concomitant breakdown of the author-driven communication system of that time. Authors were writing letters reporting their recent research results to personally selected recipients, and writing compilations of their work in the form of books. The result of this system was that relevant readers were not necessarily uniformly informed, as the information was not homogeneously shared: the research enterprise at that time got out of phase, resulting in a loss of efficacy and efficiency. Thus the birth of the journal was primarily driven by restoring efficacy and efficiency to let the research enterprise share information, with the aim of working in phase. This was assisted by technological developments at that time that allowed the deployment of an efficient distribution system in Western Europe. Thus the birth of the journal is clearly technology enabled. The Royal Society[9] took charge of the registration and certification functions by organising the editorial office, appointing Henry Oldenburg as the journal's publishing editor and having submitted articles reviewed by members of the Council of the Society. The journal itself quickly developed as the archive *per se*. The key to this breakthrough and innovative product was the decision of Mr Oldenburg to consult intensively with the most famous leading researchers of that time regarding their needs and wishes for a service. This directly led to broad acceptance.

Some of these aspects are nicely demonstrated by citations from correspondence between Oldenburg and the physicist Robert Boyle, at that time a scientific editor of the *Philosophical Transactions*; these are taken from Merton (1973). Indeed, the quotes illustrate the importance of registration for priority reasons, and emphasise the point that the archive must be lasting and useful.

Oldenburg(1): The Society alwayes intended, and, I think, hath practised hitherto, what you recommend concerning ye registring of ye time, when any Observation or Expt is first mentioned...

Oldenburg(2): have declared it again, yt it should be punctually observed: in regard of wch Monsr. de Zulichem (Huygens) hath been written to, *to communicate freely to ye Society*, what new discoveries he maketh, or wt new Expts he tryeth, the Society being very carefull of registring as well the person and time of any new matter, imparted to ym, as the matter itselfe; *whereby the honor of ye invention will be inviolably preserved to all posterity...*

Oldenburg(3): This justice and generosity of our Society is exceedingly commendable, and doth rejoyce me, as often as I think on't, chiefly upon this account, yt I thence persuade myselfe, yt all Ingenious men will be thereby incouraged to impart their knowledge and discoveryes, as farre as they may, not doubting of ye Observance of ye Old Law, of *Suum cuique tribuere.*

Boyle(1): I mightly justly be thought too little sensible of my own Interest, if I should altogether decline so civil an Invitation, and neglect the opportunity of having some of my Memoirs preserv'd, by being incorporated into a Collection, that is like to be as *lasting* as *useful.*

Forces and functions

The above description of the market and its functions aimed to provide a consistent outline of the main forces in the market required to generate knowledge and how scientific information provides dynamics in this market. The forces and functions together provide a useful description of the dynamics of the market as a whole, or the value created in the market.

The following discussion will be limited to the strategic positioning of the researcher as the main operalisation of the forces, and on this basis will elaborate the four functions in more detail, mainly from the viewpoint of changes that could be anticipated from the development towards e-science. We make use of the distinction of internal and external functions, as we have seen that only external functions can be outsourced. As this book takes a research-based view, we start the discussion with the internal functions of certification and awareness, followed by the external functions of registration and finally archiving.

Internal functions

Certification

The certification function was under continuous debate at the end of the 1980s and beginning of the 1990s (and still is), to the extent that some researchers welcomed the digitisation of scientific information as an opportunity to abandon certification or peer review. The reason was that in a transparent digital world peer review would lose its added value in helping the reader to select the right research results. The argument ran that if this function eroded, there was no longer any need to create a barrier to registration for the author. Since then, a wide variety of schemes for peer reviewing have been proposed (Roosendaal et al., 2005).

However, as we have seen, a business model is in essence the organisation of property, and in particular in the research process it is the organisation of intellectual property, next to commercial property. Core to the claim of intellectual property by the author is peer review. Claiming a scientific invention always involves peer review. The moment researchers make their scientific statements public, they register the property to these statements. By making a statement public, researchers allow the research environment to judge its scientific value. In the process of peer review the environment assesses if this contribution is worthy of further scientific effort. Peer review is thus an indispensable instrument of information production that the research environment uses to assess the quality of scientific claims in the competitive research environment.

It is particularly the certification function that is subject to different regimes or modes of doing research. Gross (1994) describes peer review as a negotiation on the level of claims permissible in a scientific article: 'The higher the level, the higher the article's status; the higher the status, the more difficult the negotiations.' And indeed, these negotiations will depend on the specific research mode the researcher is subjected to. The mode will influence the author's choice of a specific type of negotiation, i.e. a specific style of certification for the combination of content and potential application of the research being reported. It seems natural to assume that a higher necessity for autonomy of researchers is connected to a stronger emphasis on the methodological (Popper, 1963) aspects of certification, while a higher necessity for interdependence would be connected to a stronger emphasis on the potential (societal) application of the research, but without compromising on methodological standards. This means a deliberate choice for certain journals to find the right philosophy and style of reviewing papers commensurate with the research mode under which the reported knowledge has been produced, and also commensurate with the strategic and competitive position the journal occupies in the landscape of the specific market segment. Journal editors are well advised to cater for the research mode as well as the intended market segment, and consequently achieve the right visibility and recognition for their clientele, the researchers.

Merton (1973) stresses in particular the strong relation between intellectual property and the referee system. Refereeing provides a clear, authoritative system for the research enterprise, and its rules of conduct will continue to be discussed within the wider context of the goals and applicability of research (see also Daniel, 1993; Harnad's discussion forum cited in note 7). Within this context, it makes a difference if a referee, when in doubt, is inclined to accept or reject an article. Intermediate schemes are also being proposed (Zinn-Justin, 1997): referees can add comments to an article that allow the author to make revisions or, if so desired, withdraw from publication.

Quality assessment of scientific publications, whatever their mode of distribution, will remain a matter of human judgement. Technology can help by offering systems to route new findings to peers and assemble their reviews at the site where a decision is taken.[10] As publications move away from the traditional paper presentation, refereeing methods will have to evolve to deal with other media. The possibility of publishing datasets, programming codes and add-on document attachments of any size with a publication will inevitably result in increasing pressure on authors to do so. This, in turn, will exert a positive influence on the quality of publications.

Web technology makes it possible to improve the way peer review is organised. We give some examples here. *Electronic Transactions on Artificial Intelligence*[11] is a digital-only scientific journal that employs a certification system involving publication before review and (anonymous) publication of the referee reports. Readers can send in their own comments, both to the original submission and to the reviews, and all contributions are hyperlinked to constitute a small web. The web thus growing from each submission is itself a valuable source of information. Furthermore, the fact that submission and reviews are all public is expected to have a positive influence on quality. Other digital journals follow a similar strategy, especially the thriving open access journal *Atmospheric Chemistry and Physics*[12] (*ACP*), which published more than 6,000 pages in 2008 alone. The *ACP* belongs to a group[13] of journals which share the same business model. While the online journal is open access, printed copies of papers can be ordered on demand and are billed. Before a double-blind refereeing process is initiated, a submitted paper is accessible in an open online forum and can thus be discussed openly by the community. Another concept has been developed by the *Journal of Small Systems*: submitted papers go to a public online forum[14] and remain accessible. If one of the reviewers finds a paper relevant and of appropriate quality, a review will be delivered (voluntary reviewing). Once accepted for publication in the journal a paper is transferred to the journal server (see guidelines[15]). Some large international conferences have successfully used forum software, such as the Nanotube '05 Conference,[16] allowing and supporting discussion between participants on the conference abstracts. The annual Conference on Knowledge Generation, Communication and Management makes use of software allowing discussion between the referees; this greatly improves and balances the final decision and advice to authors on how to improve documents before acceptance.

Systems have been experimentally developed to assist in quality assessment by providing automated support to the comparison of experimental results reported by different sources (for a general background see de Jong et al., 1999). These systems help identify causes for divergent findings obtained in actual experiments, and also help predict what the consequences of different experimental set-ups may be. Fully quantitative simulation of experiments already yields this information, but is not always possible because our knowledge of experimental conditions is not sufficiently precise. Comparative qualitative and semi-quantitative analysis of experimental outcomes has been investigated (de Jong and van Raalte, 1999; Vatcheva and de Jong, 1999). In mathematics a rich culture has emerged of interactive textbooks.[17]

Awareness

The most complex function, awareness – the real engine in sharing information – has been tackled, in the sense that a large variety of added-value services designed to increase the awareness and selection of researchers, in particular as readers, have been created as technology allowed them.

Just as for the development of the scientific journal, awareness was the prime motivation for CERN researchers to develop the web. Promoting awareness is thus one of the main forces driving the development of web technology. One of the more compelling concepts is that of a computer-supported discovery environment (de Jong and Rip, 1997), with continuous access to the web and optimised for scientific work. In this scenario, each research group requires the competencies of a librarian to find resources of whatever form (publications, programs, videos, knowledge and databases). However, we could not find a working example of such an interactive intertwinement of library and faculty personnel.

Awareness requires communication and landmarks. Landmarks serve to alert researchers to material of potential interest. Examples of landmarks are scientific journals or websites read on a regular basis, tables of contents and review articles. A next step is to select what one is looking for from a collection or archive. This is the province of information retrieval. The past decades have seen a proliferation of approaches (see, for instance, Baeza-Yates and Ribeiro-Neto, 1999). The question of deciding between different information retrieval approaches is traditionally discussed in terms of precision and recall.[18] Such approaches as a rule leave costs out of consideration. We think the question is better approached as a microeconomic optimisation problem. For instance, improving recall only pays when the costs are lower than the costs likely to be incurred by missing relevant documents. Such problems are typically addressed by means of techniques from the field of statistical decision-making, like the use of ROC (receiver operating characteristic) curves. Dealing with the problem this way faces practical difficulties, however. It requires knowledge of the various cost factors involved: costs of indexing, of searching, of low precision, of low recall. Costs involved in indexing and searching can usually be determined with relative ease, but costs incurred by missing documents, for instance, are very hard to determine. These problems existed in the days of the paper-only environment, but the advent of digital archives has increased immensely the volume of material that can be searched and thus the problems of information retrieval. Measurements aimed at decreasing the imprecision in our current knowledge of the cost factors are urgently needed.

Full-text search methods have matured to the point that a cheap and effective solution exists for situations in which we are interested in finding only a single document or a few documents of relevance. Full-text search is cheap because the corpus is indexed fully automatically.[19] The effectiveness of full-text methods has not risen dramatically in the past years (see, for instance, the judgement of Sparck Jones, 1998), which by itself is not an argument against the method, because it has an important application domain. The main shortcoming of full-text retrieval is that it is designed for texts, and the proportion of text in scientific publications is expected to decrease. Full-text search is unable to find equations, figures, sounds or videos. Current systems for searching non-textual material mimic full-text search by finding pictures or sounds based on similarity with a query picture or sound. Such systems want the user to decide beforehand the medium in which the information is expressed. But with the proliferation of non-textual publication modes, it is unlikely that the user knows this in all or even most cases.

If we are interested in finding most, if not all, relevant documents using a search engine, there are two possible strategies.

- The author marks specific content, describing words as keywords, marks, names, title, abstract, authors, etc. in predefined and internationally agreed encoding called metadata. Thus the intentions of authors, and their or their publisher's knowledge of the Dublin Core metadata encoding performed by any search engine, allow transfer of the relevance of the information to the reader. This is now widely used. All scientific documents distributed by publishers and institutional repositories do attach metadata, which are subsequently exploited by search machines. At present, an analogous set of definitions is being discussed internationally for e-learning materials (Hilf and Mimkes, 2002). Most important are metadata for name registries and name search. A short name with some common language meaning may lead without metadata to an overwhelming number of irrelevant retrieval results (Vatcheva and de Jong, 1999).

- Alternatively, users (or their providers) select the full text and do a semantic intelligent analysis. By relations and semantic neighbourhood of words some meaning is extracted, possibly useful for searching purposes and allowing in this way retrieval of relevant related material. Some work is in progress at the Rank Xerox Research Laboratory in Grenoble within the EU European Educational Research Quality Indicators project.[20] Also, there are a number of search engines going this way. Web-related efforts employing metadata in fact return to the expensive practice of manual indexing using predefined search terms. There has been work on automating this process, but so far no working systems suitable for real-life exploitation have been demonstrated. Another development in this direction is the design of structured index terms that are more expressive than the customary flat terms (van der Vet and Mars, 1999). In some fields, such as physics[21] and mathematics,[22] structured hierarchical index terms have been developed and are in use.

One of the problems in existing information retrieval approaches is that the search space becomes too large or too complex. The user needs navigational aids, for instance virtual worlds like the now classical examples of the virtual books of Marti Hearst (1997) and the virtual music theatre developed at Twente (Nijholt et al., 1999).[23] This idea is particularly fruitful for scientific communication, where a virtual world that embodies a useful abstraction presents researchers with a familiar environment in which they can 'travel', collecting information on the way. What we mean by useful abstraction is exemplified by the illustrations published in a journal like *Scientific American.* Such illustrations are not faithful representations of reality. Rather, by means of lines, colours and other artistic manipulations, they emphasise particular aspects and ignore others. What the navigation aid will be like depends on the discipline and the task at hand. Some obvious examples include for an organic chemist, a molecular structure; for a materials scientist, a phase diagram; for a crystallographer, a model of the crystal or unit cell; for a molecular biologist, a virtual cell; and for an environmental scientist, a model of the Dutch Shallows.

Obtaining information is one step, using it is the next. Information-intensive disciplines like molecular biology increasingly rely on the availability of web-based resources like databases and programs that can be run remotely. In the course of their work, a research group will typically want to 'wire together' a set of distributed resources, both in-house and remote, to perform a particular job such as predicting the outcome of an experiment, interpreting a new finding or comparing their own findings with those reported by other groups. The lifetime of such configurations will vary between a few hours and several months. And as we have seen before, e-science will spur the development of further data-driven scientific disciplines as these become feasible, such as in social sciences.

The obstacle currently in the way of routine configurations is the multiplicity of formats. Standardisation is one way to solve this problem, but standardisation has a bad track record in many disciplines. An alternative is middleware that can be configured dynamically by feeding it a description of the resource (van der Vet, 2000). As in the far more difficult case of media conversion (discussed below), the middleware converts incoming information into a language optimised for machine manipulation, and outgoing information is converted from this internal language into the foreign format. The internal language is standardised locally, within the system and within the group that uses the system. Its symbols are defined semantically, for example in the case of molecules as standing for a bond, an atom and so on. The format of a foreign resource is precisely specified both syntactically and semantically. The syntactic specification identifies record and field delimiters and the strings that hold the information proper. The semantic specification tells how the information proper has to be converted into or from the internal format. The converters (incoming and outgoing) can be generated automatically from such a specification. If, as we expect to happen in the future, a resource provider gives access to a format specification, connecting to a resource suffices to generate a converter automatically and start downloading or uploading data in a transparent way for the user.

External functions

Registration

By reporting research results an author claims intellectual property of these results. To improve sharing scientific information, certain instruments protecting the researcher have to be developed in a publishing business model. Such an instrument is intellectual property rights. Researchers claim the property – the alternative being that the research results they produce will not exist and do not add value to scientific knowledge, and researchers themselves are not recognised for their scientific discovery. Especially in competition, intellectual property of a scientific statement is a crucial instrument. Authors claim this intellectual property by making a statement public, i.e. by publishing or registering results.

The registration has three logical steps: registration of the document for a timestamp, registration of the author, and saving this information in a paired way (registered author, registered paper).

Registration of digital material is in principle solved, but not yet implemented (Kahn, 1994).[24] Registration requires bookkeeping to keep track of who submitted a publication at which date, for which computers are ideally suited. Submission of a publication to a registration service implies that, from that moment on, neither the author nor anyone else edits the publication. This is an advantage. Authors who distribute their papers through their own websites often keep on editing them. This makes citing awkward, because it is not guaranteed that the citation remains correct or adequate over time, or possibly even the website may cease to exist. Since the citation system is one of the pillars of scientific information, the practice of constantly changing personal publications must be augmented by an archive of registered, 'frozen' publications. Modular publications are acceptable if and only if the separate modules are also properly registered separately. We will need systems for reliable authentication and timestamping, and probably also for encryption to ensure integrity of communication. Software needed for such tasks has already matured to a sufficient degree. These methods rely on the computational complexity of certain calculations, and thus become ineffective as soon as a major increase in processing speed is realised. Quantum computing in particular is held to make every current cryptographic protection method ineffective. At present there is no known replacement. All publishers serve a timestamp upon arrival of a document, which is then attached to the final publication. However, if the paper is rejected, the timestamp is lost. When the author sends it to another publisher, it gets a new and thus much later timestamp, which may be disadvantageous to eventual priority claims of the author for the results of that paper. Thus some publishers now offer a forum for papers sent in but not yet refereed (a preprint online forum), and rejected papers stay there without getting into the journal (see for example *Atmospheric Chemistry and Physics* and the *Journal of Small Systems*). A very practical solution to this problem has been adopted by the American Physical Society, which encourages its authors to send the preprint for registration to arXiv,[25] which attaches a timestamp that cannot be withdrawn and posts and archives the document forever without refereeing. The author can improve the document and hand in new versions that are archived as separate identities.

Documents which are intentionally kept dynamic and alive, e.g. kept up to date by the author, are mostly of types like technical reports or reviews of articles and books. Both may be with or without peer review. Prominent examples of peer-reviewed documents are the machine status reports of CERN, medicine research reports and the famous Living Review journals in astrophysics and other fields.[26]

Protection of intellectual ownership is strictly speaking a matter of organisation, but technology provides the means both to protect material and to circumvent protective measures. We think that a purely technical solution to the problem of protecting material is and will remain an illusion. Some systems (like Publius – see Wayt Gibbs, 2000) rely on encryption, redundancy and widely distributed storage in order to make it nearly impossible to remove material from the internet. Actually, this is the most fitting answer to the need for availability and safe archiving: to encourage readers at any library to draw and post a copy of the document. Digital copies of a digital document are clones, indistinguishable from the 'master copy', and are thus equally original.

The registration of the author has mostly been rather sloppy: either by e-mail address verification or by name. The result is that the same individual may be registered as assumedly different persons (even by a national library), according to different variations in writing his/her name, with or without second initial, different spelling variations in different languages or having changed marital status.

However, for registration of an author of an article, we do not have exactly the same requirements as for a government handing out a passport. The author may intentionally keep different pseudonyms that should be respected. But the community of readers is interested in a correct answer to the following question: is the author of a paper the same as the author of a specific other paper or not (if the author wants to release this)? And the authentication should be sempervirant and not hampered by moving or changing the e-mail address of the author.

Publishers have become alerted to this question; some, like Blackwell,[27] have started a registry. But what is needed is a cross-publishing-house solution, to find all papers of an author irrespective of the publisher. ArXiv has started to operate an endorsement service, by which authors (also of older articles, registered some time ago) can claim the authorship of their papers.

Some national institutions are operating an author identification service for their staff using a registry coupling names to a publication list (FRIDA[28] in Norway, NARCIS[29] in the Netherlands) or thesis (DissOnline[30] in Germany). Some author registries are specific to one research field, e.g. mathematics.[31] Some citation services allow authors to upload citations of their papers and thus build a personalised publication list, such as CiteULike.[32] However, what is needed is a publisher/repository-independent, international and universal author registry; one has been started by Authorclaim.[33] Once registered, authors can claim authorship of any paper, archived anywhere by anyone. They can also attach their author claim identity number to any of their future documents. This will greatly ease the work of search engines in finding relevant related papers. But there is still a long way to go to make Authorclaim or any other registry of this type a well-accepted universal service. An internationally accepted, sustainable and capable organisation is needed to run the registry, with suitable professional add-on services and effective marketing. Some concepts to achieve this were recently discussed in *The Euroscientist* (Hilf et al., 2008; Severiens, 2008).

Archiving

Careful archiving requires a sustainable deposit of material and precise retrieval – the means to find what one needs from among the archive. An extensive discussion of retrieval is given in the section on awareness, because the two are closely related.

Paper is a sustainable medium and paper journals are distributed in hundreds or thousands of copies to institutions that themselves fulfil an archival function. If even half of these institutions lost their archives, a sufficient number of copies still remain elsewhere. We can read the first *Journal des Sçavans* and the first *Philosophical Transactions* precisely because paper is such an ideal medium for archival purposes.

But the effort needed to be able to read a paper copy may well increase: distance to the only library that still has a copy may become too great; copyright may restrict the permission to read; physical effort to retrieve the volume from the paper archive in the basement may prove to be prohibitive, etc.

Long-term archiving of digital documents has a number of qualitatively different obstacles and advantages. To begin with, technically it is effortless to produce digital copies of a digital document. They are undistinguishable from the original, they are digital clones, and can be effortless transported to any place in the world and stored there. In practice, the number of servers holding the same material is mostly orders of magnitude smaller than the number of present paper archives, so the system of digital archives is more vulnerable. Thus, as a recent example, in an effort to improve long-term archiving of scientific (and other important) digital documents, the German National Library[34] signed a contract with the National Library of Australia[35] to copy reciprocally all digital material of the other country.

Also, digital material is deposited in a physical form that at best has a guaranteed longevity of 50 years. Thus the pathway to eternal archiving is to copy the digital document many times. This is done today in any computer, best by using the redundant array of independent disks (RAID) mirror technology,[36] aided by back-up policies, including remote storing of back-up tapes; and by updating hardware routinely prior to breakdown. Thus there is nowadays no concern with regard to the longevity of storage media, since their use is transitional only and in parallel.

Unlike its paper equivalent, digital content is still very often stored in a proprietary format. Proprietary formats are often replaced by newer versions, and backward compatibility is often not assured. It is internationally agreed that long-term archiving can only be realised when documents are stored in a non-proprietary and open format, meaning that all information necessary to recover a document in that format, even if relevant editors etc. are no longer in use, is known and publicly available.

Worse, the evolution of software makes information carriers and formats obsolete and practically unusable at an alarmingly fast rate. This holds for complex documents such as movies, interactive databases and computer-programmed interactions, e-learning modules, etc., where there is still a close symbiosis of content and formats, and use of proprietary software packages. Rothenberg (2000) proposes employing a system of emulators that make machines and software behave like machines and software systems of an earlier generation. The obvious criticism is that, this way, we end up with a stack of emulators on top of each other, with the risk of multiplying errors. The alternative is to convert archived documents to new formats each time the software needed for accessing the document is updated. Software for access includes not only word processors and similar but also system software like operating systems and software needed to access storage media. Therefore, this alternative in fact proposes a long chain of sequential conversion processes, so that here, too, the risk is errors stacking on top of each other. Neither way leads to long-term available, usable and readable products. Thus it is envisaged that lots of present digital e-learning material etc. will no longer be usable in the near future.

Long-term archiving policies have to ensure that even (and even more so) for complex digital information products in science and e-learning, a strict logical separation of content and format and a strict usage of non-proprietary open formats (e.g. in graphics, vector graphics) are used.

A later conversion, as noted above, is mostly too costly or simply impossible.

In summary, neither the technological nor the organisational problems in creating sustainable electronic archives are presently solved. The essential obstacle on the way towards a federated global document information system is the lack of policy for the archiving and posting of data and for document providers. For example, with regard to formats, the multiplicity of proprietary formats has proven to be utterly suited and successful for effectively and economically writing and printing administrative documents, letters, etc. However, for posting and long-term archiving it is internationally agreed that the only suitable policy (Severiens and Hilf, 2006a) is to adhere strictly to non-proprietary and fully documented formats which can be adapted in the future to any other upcoming print or screen-show formats, as projections indicate reduced availability of information. Recently, national libraries and international long-term archiving initiatives have adhered to this policy.

In Europe, several national libraries have started research programmes to tackle this problem, among them the Koninklijke Bibliotheek[37] (the national library of the Netherlands). A synoptic and extended survey of strategies leading to suitable national long-term archiving policies was presented by the German Nestor Initiative for long-term archiving in 2006 (Severiens and Hilf, 2006b).

Next to this, both publishers and universities are creating digital archives or warehouses of material under their control, allowing distribution of this information through a variety of different media. Attempts are being made to connect these archives into a more federated system. This forces the introduction of conditions for transparency, which raises the issues of responsibility for such a federated archive and its organisation.

In Germany, a coalition of universities and research libraries called DINI[38] has started the OAN[39] open access network, a project funded by the National Science Foundation to interconnect the open access data providers in universities and ensure their quality by letting them join the refereed DINI registry. In addition, to boost acceptance, a range of information services will be offered, such as citation analysis, citation extraction from open access papers, exploitation of log files, intelligent semantic analysis, etc. These services become more powerful as more data providers join the network. This scaling is an intriguing project by the digital open access community.

At present, the basic model solution being pursued is for national institutions to take over responsibility. In Germany these are DINI, with its networks and setting the rules and policies for the distributed archives, and the National Library, connected to the individual research libraries by a law-enforced obligation to archive a digital copy of all documents in their repositories. Similar developments have been seen in the Netherlands with SURF[40] and the National Library.

Will such an archive allow the author and reader to integrate information into a personal archive? This is no doubt still very much desired, and is one of the main objectives of such an archive. In the open access world the availability of information as a necessary condition to achieve this is warranted *per se*.

From Figure 5.3 we see that the archive serves as a transactional function or 'sluice' between author and reader. This raises the issue of integrating informal information into the platform of such an archive, which in turn leads to an integration of formal and informal information. This becomes particularly relevant if we take educational information into consideration as well. This means incorporating informal information into one and the same platform and management system as is used for formal communication. And it means adding metadata which describe the type of document with regard to its review status, its purpose, such as scientific publication, preprint, technical document, administrative material, notes, etc., and its addressees, such as the general public, administrators, researchers, students, etc., to allow search engines to serve different readers in different roles.

Technology

Developments have been seen to be enabled by technological progress, but their implementation has turned out to be crucially dependent on organisational changes. A brief look at what is possible and what is not, or not yet, may shed some light on the influence of technology on further developments. It is difficult to claim completeness for an overview of technological developments because computer science literature is hard to access. In older disciplines such as physics and chemistry, access is facilitated by authoritative secondary literature. In computer science, most journals are indexed that way but, unlike the case in older disciplines, journals are not the primary means of communication. For many computer science journals, the time lag between first submission and actual publication can be two years or more. As a result, a journal article is outdated when it appears and serves only archival purposes. Instead, computer researchers communicate by means of conferences and workshops with a specialised audience. A relatively large proportion of computer science publications thus become scattered over many 'grey' sources, like proceedings that often are only distributed among the workshop participants. Such publications are not indexed at all. As a result, computer science contributions are under-utilised simply because their presence is not known outside the community that produced them. Computer science contributions to scientific information are produced in many subfields that hardly communicate with each other. As such, it is a good example of the importance of organising the scientific communication process.

Hardware

An important development is the ongoing evolution of hardware. Huge amounts of data are processed in many scientific disciplines. Increased processing speed allows ever more complex calculations to be performed in reasonable time. In the longer term, novel techniques like quantum computing promise vastly increased speed. Likewise, the trend in data storage is towards larger volumes, faster access and lower prices. Here, too, novel techniques will make this trend even stronger in the longer term. As mentioned before, these developments have important consequences for the way research is carried out – the research process. They create opportunities for disciplines to become more data-driven, like in the biological sciences or social sciences. Needless to say, such a development will change the richness and reach of these disciplines, in this way opening them up for totally new areas of research.

Software

A recurrent theme in technological development is that web publishing liberates us from the limitations of the linear, mainly textual presentation of scientific findings.

Modularisation of a publication (Kircz, 1998) turns it into a small web that may include not only text and figures but also datasets, computer programs, sounds and videos. Authoring tools for such multimedia presentations will have to be developed. The author of a multimedia publication is confronted with the problem of selecting the right medium for each part of the exposition. Establishing guidelines for reasonable choices constitutes an attractive research field.

A first glimpse of what is possible may be seen in the way present editor systems try to cope with it. The LaTeX document preparation system[41] is an open source non-proprietary package that allows editing in the open non-proprietary format .tex. Texts are written in ASCII format. Style and templates are stored in separate and independently editable files; structure and layout commands are written as specific language commands, thus separating text from layout and structure. Metadata and links can be embedded; the body of information itself can be separated in subfiles which can be independently edited. Figures, video and tables can be added while remaining separate files, and a large set of different index lists (index, names, notes and various references lists) can be easily managed. It is widely used in some research fields, such as law, physics, mathematics (for which a mathematical code can be directly exported to programming machines), chemistry, where a specific encoding of chemical formulae exists, and music, where music pieces can be written. Originally it was designed to map digitally all features of the culture of book printing professionalised over centuries. LaTeX can be used with any operating system, any editor and any hardware configuration. Since LaTeX text and commands are logically separate, one can edit the text even if one has made a serious error somewhere in the command lines. One can hunt for this error separately by using the LaTeX 'debugger' (translating to a printout file) that produces a log-file with how LaTeX understands it and where errors are detected. The debugger suggests solutions to the mistake.

Because LaTeX has existed for a long time, an ever-larger community of users and freelance experts has developed worldwide who can be asked for advice; there are also numerous online guides, or ultimately one could transfer the text to the TeXdocc Center,[42] which checks it for LaTeX correctness.

Modern collaborative editing tools[43] will come more and more into use for author groups working on scientific documents, and within publishing houses, to speed and professionalise editing. While publishers might prefer the most sophisticated proprietary tool on the market, author groups, with their often quite heterogeneous background and software surroundings (editor, operating system) might prefer non-proprietary tools. The most commonly used tool today is Subversion.[44] With this, even a large group of authors can collaboratively edit or work independently and simultaneously on files and subfiles (as long as they do not edit the same line of text at the same time); it has full version control and an author does not need to be permanently online. Other tools might add an online contact with phone, TV, screen and chat modes to be able to choose media opportunistically so as to fit user needs and preferences. After all, the argument an author wants to convey can be expressed in many different ways, such as informal natural language, the semi-formal language of science, figures (including animations), simulation and spoken presentation. Within each medium there are further choices. A web publication may employ a wide range of combinations. Currently, the author dictates the choice. If readers are to select presentation style and media, tools able to convert media into each other are needed. Such tools will in most cases be unable to convert the full message from one medium into another. For instance, natural language is optimal for conveying the subtle modalities of a conclusion, while a figure is optimal for conveying a configuration. Media conversion, possibly with an information projection (Severiens and Hilf, 2006b), may well lead to a loss of information, but this may not be an issue when the loss is controlled and known to the reader. Media conversion is also a major technical problem. In a realistic scenario, it involves two conversion steps: one in which the content is converted from the original medium into some media-neutral language, and a second step in which the content is expressed in the target medium. Both steps are currently fraught with difficulties, but the second step appears easier than the first. The first step is largely unnecessary when an author distributes a publication in which large parts are expressed in some formal language optimised for machine manipulation. We therefore think that the future will see precisely such a mode of publication, allowing readers to choose media on the fly.

At present, arXiv is the oldest digital archive of scientific documents and has managed not to lose a single document for technical reasons since its start in 1991. It adheres to a strict policy only to accept documents written in an open non-proprietary format such as LaTeX, HTML or .txt,[45] and with all attached style files etc. necessary to read the document fully. Users are not permitted to submit information-projected files such as PDF or PostScript. At the choice of the reader, arXiv produces a projection, say a PDF or PostScript file. Every six months arXiv tests all documents internally to ensure long-term readability. It was found in tests (Schwander, 2002) that direct transfer from older to newer versions of read formats did not always leave the document intact – sometimes even mathematical formulae were misinterpreted.

In recent years some companies successfully registered a stripped version of their editing language package or its reading format by archiving the full programming code in a public registry – although still hidden to the ordinary reader. An example is Wikipedia.[46] Such open formats allow programmers to write conversion programs to and from LaTeX or HTML from such stripped proprietary services.

The consequences of technical development for publishing organisation and business models are not yet fully explored. But some guidelines may be noted. In the paper age, over many centuries a professional service and business model was developed and perfectly adapted to the needs of the scientific community, such that each stakeholder knew its role by heart. There was no need for contact or direct interaction and discussion between publisher and readers, or with software developers. In the digital age a new concept has yet to be found, and has to meet the needs of researchers. So a new culture of direct interaction, open discussion and listening is needed to design a robust new business model.

It is especially relevant to ensure the necessary future acceptance by the market of readers and authors, given the fact that authors and readers are as revolutionary in their research as they are conservative in sticking to their traditional and familiar means and habits of working as author or reader. The same holds for direct interaction with service developers and publishers. Such direct interaction is a prerequisite for trust and cooperation, possible outsourcing and designing new services.

Finally, with a new business model for the publishing process allowing a new distribution of roles and tasks for the various stakeholders, a new culture of interaction and communication between all partners is needed.

This holds also for the long-term archiving of scientific documents. In the paper age, journal-published papers were archived by a multitude of research and university libraries, and certainly the publisher held a copy. In the digital age, each step of the value chain in the publishing process can be performed by individual stakeholders and is decoupled from the other steps with respect to its time order – opening the possibility that each step can be performed by the best-suited and best-motivated stakeholder. This will increase and ensure the overall quality of the process. To arrive at an optimal solution for a business model, discussion, cooperation and experiments are needed.

Notes

1 See the Registry of Open Access Repositories (ROAR) cumulative graph of total number of repositories and open access documents over time at http://roar.eprints.org/index. php?prev=Prev&page=all&action=graph&format=graph&titl e=Registry+of+Open+Access+Repositories+%28ROAR%29.
2 See the ROAR website at http://roar.eprints.org.
3 The Berlin Declaration on Open Access to Knowledge in the Sciences and Humanities, made at the Conference on Open Access to Knowledge in the Sciences and Humanities, Berlin, 20–22 October 2003; see www.zim.mpg.de/openaccess-berlin/berlindeclaration.html.
4 The petition for guaranteed public access to publicly funded research results can be viewed at www.ec-petition.eu; see also Researchers of the World: Unite to Support European Commission Open Access Policy at http://openaccess.eprints. org/index.php?/archives/198-guid.html. The petition supports the proposal of the European Commission Community

Research study on the economic and technical evolution of the scientific publication markets in Europe; see http://ec.europa. eu/research/science-society/pdf/scientific-publication-study_en.pdf.

5 See the papers presented at the Euroscience 2006 seminar on Open Access: Threat or Blessing, at www.isn-oldenburg.de/ ~hilf/vortraege/esof06, and especially the talk by E. Rodrigues on the institutional open access self-archiving mandate and incentives at Universidade do Minho, at www.isn-oldenburg.de/~hilf/vortraege/esof06/esof06-rodrigues2.pdf.

6 See the University of Southampton Open Access Repository mandate at http://eprints.ecs.soton.ac.uk/.

7 See Harnad's ongoing discussion forum, Open Access Archivangelism, at http://openaccess.eprints.org/index.php; see also the complete publication list for online research communication and open access at http://users.ecs.soton.ac.uk/ harnad/intpub.html.

8 See Die Deutsche Grid-Initiative (D-Grid) at www.d-grid.de/.

9 See the archives of the Royal Society, Bodleian Library, Oxford, available at www.ouls.ox.ac.uk/bodley.

10 See, for instance, Euzenat (1995). The system described there is used to assess the quality of genome sequencing data.

11 The journal *Electronic Transactions on Artificial Intelligence* (www.etai.info) stopped operating in 2001, but the server is still active and a revival is planned.

12 *Atmospheric Chemistry and Physics* (www.atmos-chem-phys.net) is an interactive open access journal of the European Geoscience Union.

13 Meetings and open access publications (www.copernicus.org).

14 *Highlights in Small Systems* open access virtual journal and discussion forum, http://nanotube.msu.edu/HSS/ HSSguidelines.html.

15 Ibid.

16 An example of an abstract from the Nanotube '05 Conference can be found at www.fy.chalmers.se/conferences/nt05/ abstracts/K1.html; this had received 3,116 'hits' at the time of writing.

17 See the Interactive Geometry Software Cinderella, www. cinderella.de/tiki-index.php.

18 Let N be the number of documents retrieved (whether relevant or not), NR the number of relevant documents among those retrieved, and R the number of relevant documents in the entire collection. Then precision is defined as NR/N and recall as NR/R.

19 The phrase 'full-text search' embraces a range of methods that share a number of characteristics. These methods are the prime target of the yearly TREC (Text Retrieval Conference); see the TREC homepage at http://trec.nist.gov/. Indexing by means of terms taken from a predetermined list typically is not represented at TREC because such terms have to be added manually. The collections offered by TREC tend to be very large, and indexing them by hand is simply beyond the means of most research groups.

20 See the EU-funded project on European Educational Research Quality Indicators, www.eerqi.eu.

21 See the Physics and Astronomy Classification Scheme, American Institute of Physics, www.aip.org/pacs/.

22 See the 2000 Mathematics Subject Classification, American Mathematical Society, www.ams.org/msc/.

23 The Virtual Music Centre can be visited at www.seti.cs. utwente.nl/Parlevink/.

24 See digital document authentication system, US Patent 5781629, www.freepatentsonline.com/5781629.html.

25 ArXiv gives open access to e-prints in physics, mathematics, computer science, quantitative biology, quantitative finance and statistics – see http://arxiv.org/.

26 See, for example, Living Reviews in Solar Physics, http://solarphysics.livingreviews.org/, and Living Reviews in European Governance, http://europeangovernance. livingreviews.org/.

27 See the Blackwell Publishing Author Services demo version, www.blackwellpublishing.com/authordemo/default.asp.

28 Forskningsresultater, informasjon og dokumentasjon av vitenskapelige aktiviteter (FRIDA), www.ntnu.no/ub/english/ frida.

29 National Academic Research and Collaborations Information System (NARCIS), www.narcis.info/index.

30 DissOnline thesis archive and registry, German National Library, www.dissonline.de.

31 Persona Mathematica, Math-Net, www.mi.uni-koeln.de/Math-Net/persona_mathematica/.

32 CiteULike, sponsored by Springer, www.citeulike.org/search.

33 AuthorClaim registration service, http://authorclaim.org/.

34 German National Library, www.d-nb.de.

35 National Library of Australia, www.nla.gov.au/.

36 Redundant array of independent disks (RAID), http://en.wikipedia.org/wiki/Redundant_array_of_independent_disks.

37 Koninklijke Bibliotheek, www.kb.nl.

38 DINI (German Initiative for Network Information), www.dini.de.

39 OA-Netzwerk, DFG-funded project to network German academic open access institutional repositories, www.dini.de/projekte/oa-netzwerk/.

40 SURF, www.surf.nl.

41 LaTeX document preparation system, www.latex-project.org.

42 TeXdocc Center for checking LaTeX files for scientific documents, a project funded by the German Research Foundation (DFG), www.texdocc.de/info/goals.html.

43 Collaborative software, http://en.wikipedia.org/wiki/Collaborative_software.

44 Subversion open source version control system, Tigris Open Source Software Engineering Tools, http://subversion.tigris.org.

45 The transfer of proprietary formatted texts from older to newer versions, even produced by the same company, does not work correctly in many cases; and, because of the hidden proprietary format, language codes cannot be repaired by the reader.

46 Open Document, http://en.wikipedia.org/wiki/OpenDocument.

6

Criteria for business models in scientific publishing

In Chapters 3–5 we have given an extensive analysis of the research environment, the strategic positioning of the researcher and competition between researchers, and looked at specific aspects of the acquisition of scientific information in research. This was followed by an analysis of the market in terms of the relevant forces and functions, thereby covering the growth of the market and its challenges. We then focused on a comprehensive description of the four functions of certification, awareness, registration and archiving; these four functions served as a platform to discuss relevant technology developments in hardware and software.

These developments lead to considerations to be taken into account when discussing business models for scientific publishing. As outlined in Chapter 2, a business model should serve the following conditions:

- it should create value in its environment (Kurek et al., 2006) in the process at hand, i.e. the production and sharing of knowledge
- it should create a sustainable process
- it should create value for commerce.

As also defined in Chapter 2, a business model is thus viewed as the organisation of property and the exchange of property, the property being the knowledge produced by the researcher, and in particular the intellectual property of this researcher, as well as the added value of all other stakeholders.

We have chosen to follow Chesbrough and Rosenbloom (2002), in that the business model:

- articulates the value proposition
- clearly defines the market segment
- reflects the strategic position of the researcher
- identifies the value chain of scientific publishing
- reflects researchers' competitive strategy
- identifies revenues, cost structure and profit potential.

In this chapter we will use the structure provided by the business model to develop and discuss criteria for a business model in scientific publishing.

As noted in Chapter 2, any publishing business model should create value in research – the value being that it stimulates the production of knowledge by allowing researchers to share scientific information. Researchers need to share this information to be able to use it in producing knowledge. Sharing information is the main value proposition that a publishing business model should account for: it should permit researchers to make results public and acquire scientific information.

As intellectual property is the main property in scientific information, a publishing business model can only serve researchers in producing knowledge if it serves the author in claiming intellectual property and the reader in acquiring scientific information. Claiming intellectual property is effected by making research results public, with the further aim of sharing this information with colleagues and competitors in order to produce knowledge. This can only be achieved by guaranteeing adequate availability of scientific information. And acquiring scientific information depends necessarily on the availability of such information and the researchers' ability to select it. As argued in the preceding chapters, available scientific information is required by researchers for their daily research practice and their functioning in the research process. Researchers need availability of and access to scientific information anyhow, anywhere and anytime. This means no less and no more than that the information should in principle be universally accessible.

In the above, we have implicitly defined the market segment as the research environment worldwide. In the narrower sense this implies that the reader will want to acquire information and use it to do further research to produce future research results. This seems the main use of scientific information, but the information is also used in areas of application outside the original research field. Such applications can be in other research areas, interdisciplinary fields or even outside research, e.g. in societal applications in industry, services or the public at large. This means that the market segment is clearly broader than the research environment. Nonetheless, the main objective remains to share information, and it is therefore the receiving end that determines how to make use of this information for its goals and purposes. It is important to note that the value proposition is thus in principle determined by the demand side.

Serving researchers means that a publishing business model accounts for the conditions determining how researchers are conducting research. This means that the model accounts for the different modes of strategic positioning in which different types of scientific information are required, acquired and produced. This results in different behaviour in scientific publishing.

The business model in scientific publishing is determined by forces and functions, as discussed in the previous chapter, in that they describe the dynamics in the market as a whole, or in other words the value in the market. This description of the forces and functions, and in particular the functions, replaces the familiar value chain, which does not do full justice to the inherently multidimensional nature of the feedback system that we have observed while analysing the market. In discussing the functions, we have addressed outsourcing some elements of functions to intermediaries, such as publishers, libraries or others. Taking these intermediaries into account leads to different configurations of the value chain, representing different scenarios for scientific publishing that can be visualised with the familiar value chain. Looking back into history, we see that before the invention of the journal the value chain was almost entirely reduced to the author and the reader: researchers were writing personal letters to their colleagues and competitors, or even functioning as their own publisher. The journal was first introduced by the learned society as the main intermediary, later to be followed by commercial publishers for both journals and books. Some researchers thus call for a return to learned societies as publishers, as these latter are assumed to understand better and listen to researchers in their field. Other researchers advocate a return to the situation of a much-reduced value chain consisting of author and reader only. While technically always possible, and very much so in a digital environment, such a value chain would be vulnerable, but not entirely impossible, in terms of the four functions discussed in the previous chapter. Authors could publish their documents on their own web servers, and stimulate the learned society of their field to organise a peer-review report that they could attach to documents as metadata, detectable by search engines.

This concept was attractive in the early days of the web, and to some extent authors still think that way, in that they publish their publication list on the web server of their home institution and hope for the best that the professional reader finds it.

However, as time passed, more and more new and innovative web-born services came up, really helpful in finding documents in the web, organising professional printing (print on demand) and adding and identifying metadata on the document (DINI-Zertifikat, 2007) – what type of document it is, for whom it is meant, in which field, information on the authors, etc. These rich add-on services cannot be set up, developed, maintained and operated by the ordinary reader. It needs professional service providers and professional data providers. And it is not necessary for every single author or reader to become a programmer for tools. Thus the university library digital document providers, which could be such professionals, are urged to register with bodies like DINI in Germany and SURF in the Netherlands, and in this way to adhere to a set of rules to ensure professional services such as long-term archiving, long-term readability and integrity, feeding citation information into all relevant international service providers and search engines, offering author advice, etc.

A publishing business model should furthermore account for competition within the research environment, which, it is argued, affects researchers' choices, requirements and the necessary conditions for scientific information. Part of the competition is in claiming intellectual property, which evidently creates a competitive advantage for the owner of that property. But there is also a competitive element in the acquisition of information. Full availability of information can be argued to be of particular relevance to smaller research institutes, as they are necessarily more limited in their networks and generate less knowledge than larger institutes. Medium-sized and smaller research institutes may therefore be more vulnerable to limited availability of information, as this may well hamper them in producing new knowledge. Effective acquisition of scientific information also depends on the power of selection by researchers. This power, if enhanced by various services supplied by publishers, gives researchers additional competitive advantage in terms of improved access to relevant and up-to-date information acquired at the right time. As we have noted above, a business model should provide a proper balance between availability of scientific information and selection of this information by researchers. A proper balance influences the researchers' ability to acquire and select relevant scientific information, and therefore impacts on their competitive advantage.

The revenue and cost structure and profit potential in the publishing business model are dependent on the organisation of the two main dimensions that we have found in this analysis – availability and selection – or rather the balance between these two dimensions. Of course, the general rule applies that the revenue and cost structure should be commensurate, and this structure is different for an availability-driven business model and a selection-driven business model, just to mention two extreme options. A business model should also be able to create value or profit for the commercial publisher or the university acting as publisher, if so desired, but this commercial value should be commensurate with the first and foremost goal of scientific publishing: the sharing of scientific information in the service of the production of knowledge.

Last but not least, the business model should be sustainable, where sustainability is defined as the characteristic of a process, system or state that can be maintained at a commensurate level and 'in perpetuity'. As we remarked in our general discussion on business models, this boundary condition is particularly relevant in scientific publishing in its service to the production of knowledge with its strong demand for legacy. The boundary condition of sustainability means that scientific information should be available and accessible in perpetuity, while at the same time requiring a revenue, cost and profit structure that can ensure this demand. It may be noted that a subsidised and therefore political system would not only possibly render the publishing system very vulnerable, but could also endanger independent certification of the research results, in this way endangering the research process itself. Furthermore, the stakeholders in such a system might not be sufficiently motivated. Commercial enterprises would have a high motivation, if coupled to making profit, to serving a professional system, but might also be biased (in cases of publications about the market situation).

Intellectual property

To improve sharing scientific information, certain instruments protecting researchers have to be developed in a publishing business model. One such instrument to claim the property is intellectual property rights – the alternative of not claiming property, as previously discussed, is no research results, no value added to scientific knowledge and researchers being unrecognised for scientific discovery.

Especially in competition, intellectual property of a scientific statement is a crucial instrument. The author claims this intellectual property by making the statement public, i.e. by publishing. Therefore, any business model should protect this property against plagiarism and commercial abuse. Plagiarism is of direct relevance to the author, as it affects his/her paternity and integrity rights, and it is here that the author needs protection. Commercial abuse is not an issue directly relevant to authors, as they are primarily concerned that the work will be available to the scientific community, but instead highly relevant to any publisher. Plagiarism and commercial abuse thus have different addressees, and it is therefore in principle possible to split these different responsibilities.

The above argument means that protection against these two main potential infringements does not need to be in one hand, but could easily be split over different stakeholders. The university, possibly as the employer of the author or if the work is published on the university's repository or any other repository, might guarantee protection against plagiarism; in fact the university or repository has to guarantee this if the repository is freely accessible. The publisher could restrict itself to taking responsibility for commercial abuse, as this is in the publisher's commercial interest. Needless to say, the university can also be the publisher.

At present there is intense public discussion on how to realise intellectual property rights by giving them a legal frame in the digital age. Early on, derived from the needs of researchers and readers, three basic principles were formulated (Hilf, 2002a, 2002b):

- *completeness*, requiring full material (possibly as attachments) when publishing research results, with the aim of easing verification, supporting long-lasting understanding and allowing full reuse in work by other researchers

- *long-term archiving and readability*, with the aim of ensuring formats allowing long-term archiving and readability even if the technical embedding at the receiving side is different (new or other operating systems, editors, hardware media)

- *mandating free access* to a digital copy of the research material published, to ensure the broadest access without any barrier.

Equally relevant are regulations enabling a universal author identification scheme, and a legal framework setting rules for commercial activities providing the necessary add-on services (e.g. plagiarism checking, print on demand, intelligent search, etc.) for the realisation of the three principles. A legal frame requires financing these respective services for research and education.

SURF in the Netherlands has developed a concept,[1] the so-called Zwolle Principles, resulting in a collection of links, but there are more collections of copyright-activity links.[2]

In practice, in all industrial countries and the European Union political activities are under way to reform copyright law. Science organisations[3] and institutions for legislation have expressed their needs in the digital age of scientific publishing, but this must still be converted into legislation. Within the logic of this treatise it is relevant firstly to specify the needs of the research process and then to delineate concepts and requirements for commensurate services. The aim is to realise a better fit in the market, in understanding the different roles of all the stakeholders, and finally arriving at an appropriate legal framework. Summarising, agreement on the analysis and understanding of the market comes first;

trusted communication between all partners comes second; and only under such conditions is a stable legal framework for the market feasible.

As a consequence, a business model should be the enactment of the negotiation on this protection of intellectual property between researchers and other stakeholders taking responsibility for exploitation rights transferred by the researchers (Kurek et al., 2006).

Peer review

Peer review certifies the researchers' contribution to scientific knowledge and 'brands' it. In the process of peer review the research environment decides if a claim can be made and is of commensurate scientific value. Being essential for the research environment, peer review is core to any business model for scientific publishing. It serves researchers striving to be recognised in their research environment and make their results available to this environment as scientific information. Peer review also serves those doing research, especially junior researchers and students, in selecting information, as they are able to choose between different brands. In this way, peer review supports the power of selection of researchers and is important in the acquisition of scientific information.

Peer review serves the reputation of researchers. Reputable scientific journals usually have a high quality threshold, i.e. a high rate of rejections based on a consistent acceptance policy.[4] This threshold is high because in the peer-review process the journal accepts only scientific papers of a quality commensurate with the scope and standards of the journal. As mentioned in Chapter 4, researchers competing for recognition do not want to publish in journals they consider to be of doubtful quality; thus low standards will be detrimental to audience and revenue stream (Prosser, 2005). Therefore, peer review should be a basic service included in any business model for scientific publishing.

However, peer review is not uncontested. Next to its strengths, as outlined above, peer review also shows some weaknesses. A main weakness is that review takes time, sometimes a very considerable amount of time, often resulting in severe publication delays. Peer-review throughput times have been seen to be dependent on the scientific discipline, and some disciplines, such as mathematics, are known for their rather long throughput times. In some disciplines this is even desirable, as the claim has been made by submitting the paper and a prolonged throughput time for peer reviewing is considered to result in competitive advantage for the authors of the paper, while in other disciplines throughput times are as short as possible, e.g. in some physics areas. As stated, these delays may be commensurate with the strategic positioning the authors strive for, but quite often the delays are due to inefficient management by the editors of the journal. The method of peer review also depends on the discipline. In general peer review is blind, i.e. performed anonymously by the reviewers; sometimes it is double blind, i.e. the authors and affiliation are hidden for the reviewers and the reviewers are hidden for the authors. This is the case in many medical sciences. In some disciplines one reviewer is considered sufficient, e.g. in many physics and chemistry areas; in other fields such as mathematics, medicine and social sciences two or more reviewers are requested.

Whereas a longer throughput time may give the authors a competitive advantage with respect to their direct colleagues, it also means a competitive advantage for reviewers, who have advanced knowledge with respect to their colleagues. Reviewers can even reject publication, with the goal of gaining competitive advantage over a direct competitor. Although direct proof is not available, there is a widespread belief that such practices sometimes happen, leading to researchers having low trust in the peer-review process (see e.g. Daniel, 1993). In some areas such as high-energy physics peer review is often viewed as redundant, as the community is relatively small and papers are circulated as preprints to this community, e.g. through the Los Alamos archives, in this way making a claim prior to publication. Nonetheless, these papers are published in established journals, and this latter publication is considered the authentic paper, properly peer reviewed according to the standards of the journal. In this way, possible obstruction or even plagiarism by reviewers is counteracted by the transparency of the preprint system.

Another topic in peer reviewing is the twigging of research into ever-expanding interdisciplinary or multidisciplinary fields. Many papers of this nature have a hard time getting accepted by disciplinary journals, as they either fall beyond the scope of these journals or are rejected by disciplinary reviewers because the reviewers are not familiar with the interdisciplinary developments and have limited competence in these new fields. Actually, it takes considerable time to establish a reliable reviewers' pool for newly developed fields, as was clearly demonstrated in the end of the 1980s with the sudden expansion of the field of high-temperature superconductivity. It took at least a year to establish a broadly agreed review code for this field.[5] This hampers the development of such a new field and leads to founding new journals, in this way contributing to a further proliferation of research journals. And indeed, this twigging is one of the main reasons for the expansion in the number of journals we have witnessed over time.

As stated before, the essence of scientific communication is that 'authors want to publish more, readers want to read less' (Roosendaal et al., 2005; Geurts and Roosendaal, 2001; Roosendaal and de Ruiter, 1990; Roosendaal et al., 2008). This statement emphasises the argument that researchers want wide exposure for their work and at the same time they want to select the information relevant for their work effectively and efficiently. This information has to be available, up to date, relevant and easy to find. The acquisition of scientific information depends on the power of selection by researchers. This selection depends on the researchers' ability to assess the relevance and quality of information. This power can be enhanced by specific pre-selection services to disclose the information effectively and efficiently. Researchers do thus require 'basic' services making certified, i.e. peer-reviewed, scientific information generally available.

Notes

1 Copyright Management for Scholarship, http://copyright. surf.nl/copyright/.
2 Urheberrecht in der Informationsgesellschaft; Institut für Urheber- und Medienrecht, www.urheberrecht.org/topic/Info-RiLi/.
3 In Germany the Coalition for Action: Copyright for Education and Research (Aktionsbündnis Urheberrecht für Bildung und Wissenschaft, www.urheberrechtsbuendnis.de) has a membership of large science organisations, 363 learned societies and institutions and 7,000 leading figures in the science area. In Europe 27,500 people have signed a petition to the European Union for guaranteed public access to publicly funded research results; this follows an EU study on the economic and technical evolution of scientific publication markets in Europe.

4 Statistics of the *Academy of Management Journal*, www.aom. pace.edu/amjnew/journal_statistics.html.

5 Discovered in 1986, high-temperature superconducting immediately got the Nobel Prize in 1987, but specific journals came much later – see http://en.wikipedia.org/wiki/High-temperature_superconductivity.

7

Scenarios for scientific publishing

Following the logic of this book, business scenarios for scientific publishing should be tested in their ability to fulfil the boundary conditions for business models in terms of value proposition, market segment, strategic positioning, value chain, competition, revenue and costs structures and profit potential. In Chapter 6 we restricted the discussion to the criteria demanded by researchers as the primary stakeholders in scientific publishing. This is a valid approach, as these constitute criteria from the research point of view for success of a particular business model and can therefore be used to test the suitability, acceptability and feasibility of the model for the main stakeholder, the user of the system – researchers as authors, readers or both. This should not and cannot necessarily mean that the scenarios are also suitable, acceptable and feasible from the viewpoint of the other stakeholders, the intermediaries in the process, as this will depend on their goals and objectives as well as the restrictions they have, such as in terms of resources. Only when these specific restrictions are known can a scenario be judged on its suitability, acceptability and feasibility for the specific stakeholder.

Therefore, we will restrict our discussion of scenarios to testing these on the basis of the business model conditions set by the research environment. These conditions are evidently not restricted to this environment, but should also include the wider societal environment as far as it is of relevance to the research environment. And indeed, the boundary conditions of the research environment really matter, for researchers and for all other stakeholders.

We have seen that, for researchers as authors, making research results public with the objective of claiming intellectual property is most relevant. Making results public means they are widely available and accessible to anybody who could possibly take an interest in these results. It goes without saying that authors want to be in command of which results they make public, including data and other information, and of the timing of the process. For competitive reasons researchers have as a main driving force clearly articulated demands with respect to important business considerations, such as the speed of publication once the publishing decision has been taken.

Likewise, for researchers as readers wide availability and accessibility are boundary conditions in being able to select results needed for their goals, be this research or other applications; they also need appropriate and affordable selection tools. For the same competitive reasons it is here relevant that research results are available at the right time. In particular, researchers from small or medium-sized research groups or institutes are highly dependent on proper and timely access to results if they compete with researchers from larger or richer institutions or want to participate in larger-scale projects, as they probably have to do in order to remain in phase with their colleagues. And for sheer competitive reasons, remaining in phase is a *conditio sine qua non*. An important parameter to the speed of publication is the speed of certification, of peer review. By the same token it is widely acknowledged that being a reviewer gives researchers a definite competitive advantage over their colleagues, requiring very strict conditions on the speed and quality of the review process and the publication process as a whole. Again, it should be the researchers who are in control of the process.

We have noted that the market segment is largely determined by the receiving end. It is in the interests of researchers that their results are as widely available as possible, but this demand for availability will be different for a Mode1, Mode2 or Mode3 researcher. In particular, Mode3 researchers, and to a somewhat lesser extent Mode2 researchers, are in need of wide exposure in their societal environment, as in this way they can create demand for their products. This can be achieved by making the original results available to wider audiences or by appropriate tertiary publishing instruments, but with the condition that these will be available at the same time as the primary instruments. This will lead to new dynamics in the process.

In line with the above, it seems useful to analyse the business model in terms of strategic positioning, i.e. along the modes reported for researchers. Strategic positioning is especially noticeable in the market forces discussed earlier (Chapter 5), in particular the forces of availability and selection. As we have noted, the goal for researchers in the market of scientific communication is recognition by the relevant community, and strategic positioning, including competition, is the integration force in this respect. Recognition is achieved in a combined effort of availability coupled with aspects of the speed of publication, and here the speed of the reviewing process is an important element, plus finding the right market segment for the research results, or in other words the audience of the publication outlet.

Taking these four elements of availability, selection, speed of publication and the choice of audience, or market segment, we are able to see differences in criteria for business models for the three relevant typical research modes we have described.

Looking at Mode1, we observe that the availability of material can be restricted to research information proper, without mixing this with information about research management and the like or any information about possible applications, i.e. details of the potential societal environment of interested companies, communities or even government. Mode1 researchers are less dependent on their colleagues in the selection of material to be acquired from the research environment, and even less from the wider societal environment. Speed of publication is desired to be commensurate with the mores of the research environment but should be competitive from the research point of view. The audience is primarily restricted to the research environment proper, as there is no direct need to satisfy societal demands.

In contrast, Mode2 researchers will be more dependent on broader information from their direct and indirect colleagues, and also for reviewing results, and are much more dependent on information from the societal environment, represented by company interests, funding agencies, local communities and the like. Selection strategies are very much influenced by the researchers' colleagues as information sources having control over what they want to share. Mode2 researchers need to be aware of related societal needs from more public sources in order to pursue projects that will cater to specifically articulated societal demands. The societal environment may wish to delay or sometimes inhibit publication of part or even all the results, in this way influencing the authoring and final content of publications. Mode2 researchers supply on the demand of the societal environment, sometimes coinciding with interests articulated by the research environment, leading to publication of results or reports for special target groups, sometimes even of a confidential nature. These activities are quite laborious and will have a direct and negative impact on the productivity of Mode2 researchers.

Looking now at Mode3 researchers, we see that in terms of availability the demands are very similar to those of Mode2 researchers. In selection strategies the emphasis will be on using colleagues for enhancement, with the clear objective of creating demand in the wider audience of the societal environment for the researchers' potential scientific results and products. Publication is not influenced by the environment, but writing can be somewhat slowed down, as larger alliances are needed for a single publication requiring more management time, in particular for strategic positioning. Mode3 researchers will seek to collaborate with a broad variety of disciplines to increase the dynamics of the research process. For these reasons, Mode3 researchers will seek a broad audience comprising researchers lending scientific authority in the wider societal environment, research councils, government, industry, etc. In addition to scientific publications, they will use dissemination channels such as newspapers, websites and special editions for popularising science. Research publications then function as the ultimate authoritative resources, therefore requiring a high speed to market.

Next to these considerations on the market forces as expressed in the different research modes, the market for scientific publishing has been seen to be very dynamic; its dynamics are well described by the four functions of certification, awareness, registration and archiving. These functions have been chosen to be invariant of the publishing environment, be this paper or digital. An important issue in scenarios is the degree of intermediation or disintermediation that will be required to make up a good business scenario. A relevant boundary condition in these considerations is that scientific publishing is, and probably should not be, a core research activity, even if it is, as we have seen, of prime relevance to the research process. This means that the added value of intermediaries will be measured in terms of added value to the research process. Adding value means freeing up precious research time, rather than spending time and efforts on non-core activities and slowing down the production of knowledge. The main parameters to judge this added value are the degree of availability and accessibility, the speed of publication, the speed and quality of the peer-review process and the ability to select the right information at the right time with least effort. And it is up to researchers, as authors and readers, if they are willing and can afford to pay for these services. The revenues and costs, and consequently the profit potential, will differ for different scenarios, be these driven more by availability or selection. It is in the authors' opinion well acknowledged that in publishing there is no free lunch; moreover, the requirement for long-term sustainability requires commensurate profits in the entire publishing process.

Summarising, we have noted that any publishing business model should be concerned with a proper balance between the two indispensable parameters of availability and ability to select. The ability to select can be separated into basic selection based on the structure of scientific information, such as editorial lists or journal titles, and enhanced selection determined by added-value services. Also indispensable is protection of intellectual property, as this is the core of any business model, and peer review is core to this property. Healthy profits are required to ensure sustainability of the system, as sustainability is a *conditio sine qua non* for the research process.

We have also noted that the basic services including peer review and basic selection and value-added services including enhanced power of selection are in principle two distinct services. These distinct services can therefore in principle be provided by two separate suppliers: one responsible for wide availability of scientific information and one for the enhanced power of selection by researchers. Google might serve as a possible example.

A publishing business model can then allow different combinations of availability and power of selection. This leads to a suite of different business models for scientific publishing in which availability and selection can in principle be provided by different combinations of suppliers.

In this way responsibilities and costs for availability can be kept separate from responsibilities and costs for selection. These models allow researchers to acquire selected information and choose services for which they want to pay additionally.

Separating these costs will ultimately be of benefit to researchers. Paying for basic services in combination with added-value services provided by just one supplier makes publishing and the acquisition of information quite expensive, and thus increases the competitive difference between large and small research institutes. Having different options by paying separately for chosen services encourages researchers to publish scientific information in or acquire scientific information from a medium providing such options.

In these models, researchers claiming intellectual property pay only for the fundamental services of availability, peer review and basic selection. In addition, researchers acquiring

117

information can buy services according to their current needs, determined by their strategic and competitive position. Different types of scientific information and different situations may well require different added-value services, even for an individual researcher.

A solution for such business models could be a federated network of repositories (Roosendaal, 2004). Such a network would provide availability of scientific information and in this way fulfil researchers' need for recognition and access to relevant scientific information. It could also cut costs for availability and additional services from different sources for researchers acquiring scientific information, as well as costs for claiming the property for researchers. Intellectual property and the protection of the author's moral rights have been seen to be an important element of a business model (Zalewska-Kurek et al., 2008). Repositories will only be successful if they are willing to warrant these moral rights of authors.

A business model in which the costs of availability and selection are combined in one package is the subscription model. This model provides limited availability of scientific information, as access to the information is restricted by a subscription fee. This fee is usually paid by the research environment via a library. The model aspires to maximum availability, albeit bounded by selection. Selection is in this way used as an ordering principle to create this bounded availability. Limited availability adds to this. A library has limited financial resources and therefore has to make choices about what scientific information to buy; individual researchers have no say in the matter. This limited availability is the clear weakness of this model from the viewpoint of the researcher. On the other hand, the researchers' power of selection is enhanced by the publisher offering additional services (ibid.), such as abstracting and indexing, sophisticated search software, appropriate metadata, alerting systems, mailing lists, etc., above the basic services, including peer review, being paid for by the researcher acquiring scientific information via a subscription fee.

The discussion about business models can be illustrated using a value chain representation. Figure 7.1 presents the chain of added values in the subscription model. The essence of this model is that the acquisition, and thus selection, of scientific information precedes its dissemination.

A variation on the subscription model is a licence agreement between a consortium of libraries and a publisher. Although the initial licence agreements provided overall access to the entire publishing list of the publisher with which the agreement was signed, such a licence agreement is still a subscription model – as was shown recently, when publishers wanted to limit access to new subscription units composed of certain packages of journals, thereby again intending to restrict the overall availability of the information. Thus the licence agreement is not fundamentally different from the subscription model.

The open access model as an alternative publishing model can be analysed in terms of availability and selection. The

Figure 7.1 The subscription model

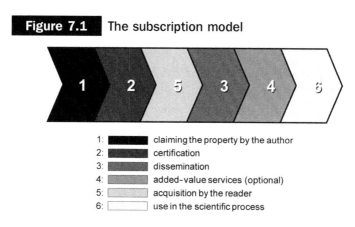

1: claiming the property by the author
2: certification
3: dissemination
4: added-value services (optional)
5: acquisition by the reader
6: use in the scientific process

goal of open access is to provide general availability. There are variations in open access models, but the basic principle is that researchers as authors claiming intellectual property pay in some way or another for the publication. This enables sharing scientific information, as the information is available and accessible free of charge anywhere and anytime. This means in practice that researchers are not dependent on the choice of a library. But, at the end of the day, it is always the scientific community that pays for the publication – in the subscription model it is the reader channel via library funds, and in the open access model the author channel via research funds. A premise to the open access model is that authors can access funds to cover these costs, be this directly or via the institution in the form of a publication budget. This may require a transfer of funds from the library budget to a publication budget. This is in principle possible, as the library budget would be freed from subscription responsibilities; however, increases in subscription prices have been seen to be barriers to such a transfer. Nowadays, technology allows open access journals to offer most of the abovementioned selection services. A clear weakness of this model is that there is no real incentive to enhance the reader's power of selection.

Another issue in relation to the open access model is that there is some fear that peer review may be weakened (Prosser, 2005). Analysing the subscription and open access models in terms of the four functions of scientific publishing points out that the problem is the potentially lower reliability of the peer-review process because the researcher pays to be published. For the same reason of reliability, the university acting as publisher cannot manage certification of research results produced by its own employees (Roosendaal, 2004).

The open access model is presented in Figure 7.2. The basic idea of the model is that scientific information is available to any reader, who acquires the information either with or without added-value services such as sophisticated search software, appropriate metadata, alerting systems, mailing lists, etc.

It is sometimes remarked that the open access model is not a business model but a distribution model, using the argument that in open access the information is available and accessible free of charge to the reader. However, as we have seen it is the scientific community that pays for making the research results public, meaning that there is a monetary currency of exchange. But even if this monetary exchange could theoretically be reduced to zero, the distribution model would be just a special kind of business model. It is, furthermore, doubtful if such a model can be sustainable at all.

Some publishers have introduced an open access model where libraries pay for authors to be able to publish a certain number of works in journals of the contract publisher. Access to this publisher's journals is also free of charge. As the allotted number of publications is restricted in time, such a model turns out to be a variation on the

Figure 7.2   Open access model

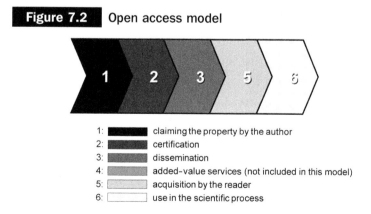

1: claiming the property by the author
2: certification
3: dissemination
4: added-value services (not included in this model)
5: acquisition by the reader
6: use in the scientific process

subscription model, in particular if the allotted number of publications cannot be delivered in time.

Combining the costs for the two parameters of availability and selection thus always results in a weakness in one of the two main parameters. We see that neither the subscription model nor the open access model does entirely fulfil the necessary conditions for general availability and power of selection at the discretion of researchers. Each of these models focuses too much on one parameter.

Restricted availability and accessibility give larger and strategically resourceful research institutes competitive advantage over smaller institutes, groups or individual researchers. This means that some researchers are excluded from scientific results. This is not in line with the Mertonian (1973) ethos of science. Therefore, the open access model has been seen in the last decade as more acceptable in the research habitat and more suited to the necessary conditions for scientific information because it provides a free flow of scientific information.[1] The open access model thus seems to be more acceptable than the subscription model, as it complies with the competitive goals of researchers in claiming intellectual property and acquiring information, but it still has the weakness that the power of selection may be less advanced.

The open access model requires a publication budget. In the absence of a full switch to open access, a research and higher education institution also requires a library budget. This may well explain why open access is to date only successful in high-cost research environments.

An example of a model providing full basic services combined with optional added-value services is presented in Figure 7.3, showing a basic, no-frills service of sheer availability coupled with peer review as the major value

Figure 7.3 Optional business model with added-value services

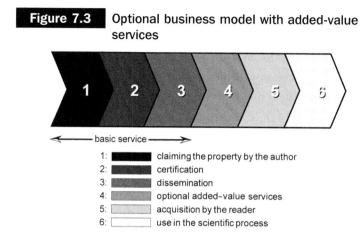

basic service

1: ■■■■■ claiming the property by the author
2: ■■■■■ certification
3: ■■■■■ dissemination
4: ■■■■■ optional added-value services
5: ☐ acquisition by the reader
6: ☐ use in the scientific process

proposition required, and with optional value-added services as the reader might desire.

Separating these costs benefits researchers. Paying for basic services and all added-value services provided by only one supplier may make publishing and acquisition prohibitively expensive, and in this way increases, as we have seen above, the competitive difference between large and small research institutes.

In these models, researchers claiming intellectual property pay only for the basic services of availability and peer review. Furthermore, researchers acquiring information can buy services according to their current needs, determined by strategic positioning and competition. Different types of scientific information and different situations require different added-value services. As an example of unconventional business models allowing a specific scientific subcommunity free access to documents, we can mention SCOAP3,[2] a coalition of commercial publishers and high-energy physics research institutions and societies set up to ensure free access for its community to all relevant documents in all journals of the involved publishers. The

Cochrane Collaboration organising the Cochrane Library[3] may serve as another example.

From the above discussion, we see that a model providing full basic services combined with optional added-value services fits the necessary conditions for scientific information better than either the subscription model or the open access model. It would therefore be interesting to consider such a model in the future development of scientific communication, in particular as the model is fully flexible at the demand side of the reader.

Notes

1   See, for example, *Serials Review: Special Issue on Open Access*, 2004, www.sciencedirect.com/science/journal/00987913.
2   SCOAP3 (Sponsoring Consortium for Open Access Publishing in Particle Physics), www.scoap3.org.
3   Cochrane Library, http://www3.interscience.wiley.com/.

8

Consequences for stakeholders

Following the arguments in this book, it becomes evident that scientific information has been dominated over many decades of the paper age by one business model: the subscription model. It is only recently, with the advent of the digital age, that an alternative concept has been proposed, open access, but to date it has had limited although slowly increasing success. Its success is considered limited in that the uptake of the model in the market is slow as compared to the penetration of really successful business model innovations. This slow uptake can only be the result of the fact, addressed in this book, that there are no convincing incentives for the stakeholders involved. A clear sign of this is that the open access business model concept is experimenting with an ever-increasing variety of specifications to find a long-term, stable and feasible solution for its financing.

Inspecting the dominant subscription model further, it also becomes clear that this model is heavily supply-oriented while providing bounded or limited availability, and thus is in principle a publisher-centred model but focusing on the author as the primary stakeholder for consideration. The open access model in all its variations coming up in the market is in essence also a supply-oriented model. Again, like the subscription model, it is primarily a publisher-centred model, in particular in its forms of open access mandates for publishing on an institution's repository followed by subsequent publication in a journal. This means that both known business models in their different manifestations in the market are essentially supply-oriented and publisher-centred, whereas the analysis in this book, based on the philosophy of convergence of the scientific information market towards e-science, results in a business model that should be demand-oriented and above all research-centred. Central to this analysis are the four market forces of recognition, competition, availability and selection that arise from analysing researchers in both the wider societal environment and the research environment proper, and in particular from analysing the strategic position and competitive advantage of researchers and the four market functions of certification, awareness, registration and archiving (Chapter 5). Both forces and functions have been seen to be invariant for technological changes or even disruptions.

In this discussion, 'demand-oriented' means that the business model should fulfil the demand of authors for full availability and the demand of readers to decide on their own needs for selection depending on the information they want to acquire. 'Research-centred' means that the business model should allow for the different strategies researchers want to develop in their strategic positioning in the relevant environments and competing in these environments. The business model should comply with the prime demand of sharing scientific information for the benefit of research, i.e. sharing information in a very dynamic environment demanding that information is made public and can be fully acquired.

Most important is that a business model furthers research and teaching in meeting all requirements of these environments. This is the essence of being research-centred, as reflected in the value proposition of the business model. While research and teaching are the core activities of research and higher education institutions, by the same token it does not seem wise to make the distribution of scientific information a core activity of these institutions. This implies that the research community should be at the heart of the organisation of scientific information, but at the same time many activities can and should be outsourced to third parties, be these commercial or not. This calls for a sound alliance between all parties concerned – research institutes, publishers, libraries and other intermediaries in the value chain, each with their own needs for organisational autonomy and strategic interdependence. And, indeed, we have to analyse these relations in the same way as we analysed the relations between researchers and the environment in Chapter 3 (Figure 3.1), but now taking the research environment as the relevant environment for the other stakeholders involved.

Strategic positioning of stakeholders

In this section we will analyse the strategic positioning of the main stakeholders in the production of scientific information along the dimensions of the necessity for organisational autonomy and strategic interdependence. This means that we look at the production of scientific information as an alliance or a sort of integration of these main stakeholders into the research environment. We can visualise this integration in a similar way as we did in

Figure 3.1 for the relation between researchers and the environment. This visualisation results in Figure 8.1.

In previous chapters we used the model of Haspeslagh and Jemison (1991) to analyse the strategic positioning of researchers as an organisation, i.e. as individual researcher, research group or research institute, in the environment. In doing so we adopted the terminology used in policy studies in using the term *mode* to characterise a specific type of positioning. As we now turn to analysing the strategic positioning of organisations like universities, libraries, publishers and other stakeholders, and the degree of necessary integration between these organisations, we will return to the original terminology used by Haspeslagh and Jemison in their analysis of integrating two organisations. An integration characterised by low necessity for organisational autonomy coupled with high necessity for strategic interdependence would call for absorption of one organisation into the other; high necessity for organisational autonomy coupled with high necessity for strategic interdependence would call for a symbiotic relation between the organisations; high necessity for organisational autonomy coupled with low necessity for strategic interdependence would call for preservation of both

Figure 8.1   Different types of integration

| | | Necessity for organisational autonomy (OA) | |
		Low	High
Necessity for strategic interdependence (SI)	Low	Holding	Preservation
	High	Amalgamation	Symbiosis, intertwinement

organisations; and finally low necessity for organisational autonomy coupled with low necessity for strategic interdependence results in a holding relation between the organisations.

As stated before, we look at the relations of stakeholders such as the library, the publisher and other intermediaries with the research environment, as this ensures that a business model for the production of scientific information will be research-centred and demand-oriented. These existing relations in the market are characterised by a high degree of subsidiarity, implying that stakeholders enjoy a high degree of strategic interdependence.

Looking at the library, we note in particular the development towards e-science requires scientific information to be fully integrated into research. In performing its future functions there is no high necessity for organisational autonomy for the library, but there is clearly high necessity for strategic interdependence with research. No doubt there is a location-bound autonomy needed for the hard-copy archives, but this does not demand full organisational or managerial autonomy. This leads to the conclusion that the library can in principle be absorbed into the research organisation and should be managed as an integral part of research. In a research and higher education institute a library also functions in teaching. However, the requirements for disseminating teaching information are not much different from those for research information, whereas we have seen the need for further convergence in the development towards an e-science environment. Absorption of the library by research can only stimulate this development.

For the publisher we have observed that the distribution of scientific information, and in particular the added-value services coupled to selection, call in the publisher's relation with research for high necessity for organisational autonomy coupled to a high necessity for strategic interdependence, as the publisher's products are produced by and for the research community. This leads to the conclusion that publishers and research should establish a symbiotic relation for the long-term benefit of both parties. We have seen that in principle the basic services in the distribution of scientific information can be split from the value-added services, and as a consequence different organisations can take responsibility for these different services. Basic services include peer review, which has been seen to require independence from research, meaning an organisation in addition to research-held repositories. Such an organisation could well be managed by research, or alternatively by independent publishers, e.g. commercial publishers or learned societies, provided that they respect the need for a symbiotic relation with the research environment warranting a research-centred business model.

Similar arguments lead to similar conclusions for the relation of the other intermediaries in the production of scientific information, albeit that their own relation with the publisher could well be stronger than symbiotic, as their necessity for organisational autonomy with respect to the publishers will not be that high. This could well result in a convergence of intermediaries and publishers, finally leading to full absorption.

The symbiotic relation between the research and the publishing environments, i.e. publishers and other intermediaries, requires a sort of virtual organisation composed of these two environments so as to ensure steady progress in the development towards e-science. In fact, it calls for an organisation similar to one we know well from the development of the World Wide Web: the WWW Consortium (W3C). In this way, a worldwide scientific information network as described in the vision could be realised with a dispersed spectrum of stakeholders, ensuring a diversified and differentiated network that is optimally integrated in research and teaching.

The above discussion addresses the question of the future structure and organisation of the scientific information market. We noted before that in the present market research has outsourced a number of functions or tasks to other stakeholders, such as publishers, libraries, agents, etc., or 'insourced' to institutions such as learned societies, universities or research and education institutions. This accounts in particular for the external functions of registration (publisher, learned society) and archive (publisher, library), and the logistics aspects of the internal certification function (publisher, learned society).

No doubt these considerations will affect the balance in the market, and particularly the certification function. Changes in the certification function will translate into changes of the registration and archive functions. In the end, this will affect the possible schemes and degrees of outsourcing.

A major issue in this development is wide acceptance by the main stakeholders, the researchers as users. A condition to achieve wide acceptance by users of such a network is that it provides access to a critical mass of information material in their specific research subject. Critical mass is also needed to be able to support a variety of business models for the information market. These different business models can represent different organisational and legal models, as individual stakeholders will need this flexibility to compete effectively with their information products. Next to critical mass, this necessary reorganisation of the whole chain of information management requires a stable, adjusted frame of legal bodies, and thus new specific laws.[1]

The network should thus be able to support a comprehensive variety of business models that can and will be agreed between the different stakeholders for different classes of information and different ways to access the content in this network. A main requirement of the network, then, is that no feasible business model now or in the future should a priori be ruled out or be in principle impossible. But, as we have seen, a business model can only be feasible if it is research-centred and demand-oriented.

The general aim is to make research and educational content widely available in a coherent way, complementing the objectives and aims of e-science initiatives. Users will want to have access to research and teaching resources in a coherent manner using an information environment that can be shared comfortably. In such a network this access will be possible without relocating the information in intermediate repositories for reasons other than strictly technical. Thus researchers, teachers and students should be able to access and find a wealth of online resources across institutions and publishers.

As we have stated before (Roosendaal et al., 2005), the implementation of the vision will affect the research and higher education institution in many aspects: in research and the research process, in teaching and the teaching process, in its organisation and in its technical competencies. It may well have legal consequences for intellectual property; it may well change the role of the institution in the entire information landscape and its proprietary roles in both research and education organisation and techniques. We are already witnessing some if not many of these changes.

This will affect the strategic position of institutions as important stakeholders in the scientific information market. The positions of intermediaries in this market, such as publishers, libraries, agents etc., will change concomitantly, as we have seen in the above analysis.

As an initial reaction to these changes we have already witnessed a convergence of the roles of publishers, libraries and agents in their attempts to cater for the entire intermediary function of each of these stakeholders. And many research and higher education institutions and other knowledge-intensive organisations and companies worldwide are presently developing novel but most often disparate approaches to creating repositories.

The creation of a cohesive and coherent network should allow and guarantee the best return on investment, in whatever form, for all stakeholders on their own terms, be they public (such as institutions) or private (such as publishers) organisations. It is in the interest of each individual stakeholder to strive for maximum flexibility in the marketplace. This can best be achieved by organising the market in such a way that it allows maximum compliance with the vision in the marketplace.

Detailed consequences for the individual stakeholders have been extensively discussed in a previous book (Roosendaal et al., 2005). To make the present book comprehensive, we will repeat in the remainder of this chapter some of these consequences without claiming originality of these ideas.

Users

In this book we have taken the premise that scientific information should serve the production of knowledge. On this basis we have attempted to develop a consistent philosophy resulting in the demand for a research-centred and demand-oriented family of business models for scientific information. These business models would ensure further integration of scientific information into the research and teaching enterprise in its development towards e-science. Moves towards e-science have been observed by Heimeriks and Vasileiadou (2008) in ICT-related differences in recent developments in the formal publication system. New formats for online journals have destabilised the institutionalisation patterns of formal scientific publication by opening up the sphere of production, publishing and diffusion to smaller-scale participants, such as individual researchers or small scholarly societies, and opening up new issues for a renegotiation of power between researchers and publishers on copyright management and new filtering mechanisms. Heimeriks and Vasileiadou (ibid.) observe further that although the digitisation of the journal system has opened up new options, these have not stabilised in most scientific fields. Digital publishing seems to have provided an additional layer of communication rather than destabilising the role of existing journals. This is no doubt because the business model employed is still the dominating subscription model from the print age, as we observed in Chapter 2.

Research and HE institutions

The institution is a most important knot in the scientific information network. Information provision is a strategic activity of the institution in the service of research and teaching. Institution managements have become aware of their responsibility for providing adequate information services. Examples of this awareness are the declaration by the German Rectors Conference (HRK)[2] of November 2002, the integration of information provision programme started by the German Research Council (DFG),[3] the DARE project[4] in the Netherlands, activities in the UK, driven by the Research Councils,[5] and at some universities in the USA, notably the mandate for open access at Harvard University (de Rosnay, 2008), which is an 'opt-out' policy[6] (local authors have to apply in paper for an individual opt-out from the regular mandate to archive a digital copy of new research documents in the Harvard Institutional Repository), and in the UK, where a national charity organisation, the Wellcome Trust,[7] mandates open access for all documents when the research has been funded by the trust. A further example of the awareness of the academic world is the Berlin Declaration[8] of German academia.

The emerging institutional repositories play a significant role in creating a scientific information network, in particular as they are augmented by standards-based mechanisms such as the OAI,[9] Open URL,[10] etc. enabling the indexing of scientific information on a global scale. These repositories bring several improvements in response to the needs identified:

- they meet the preference of researchers to use their own institutional facilities to access digital content
- they improve access to digital content by increasing the number of journal articles and datasets which are freely available
- they maintain standards of academic quality through the authority of the institution and by enabling normal peer-reviewed publication to continue alongside archiving in an institutional repository.

In order to ensure general availability of scientific information, a number of organisational issues are relevant:

- strict organisation of information management at the institution
- new divisions of labour and collaboration schemes in research
- in teaching, a new division of labour in creating teaching material and coaching students
- enhanced mobility of students
- integrated management systems (above all else).

In summary, high-value information provision is a strategic core activity of every institution, and becomes even more relevant in the development towards e-science.

Libraries

The research and higher education institutions are the natural candidates to initiate the development of new business models and structures. As we have seen, this is foremost an organisational and not a technical challenge. The result of our analysis is that the major organisational challenge will be to absorb the library into the research organisation, and institutions and libraries have the task of initiating this process.

The goal of this absorption is to change the relation between the institution's primary processes and the information provision for these processes. It has been seen that this information provision will have to integrate more closely with the primary processes to deliver the services they need. This absorption no doubt requires a delicate integration strategy at the institution's top management level.

As a consequence of our arguments, the institution will develop itself further into an active and professional manager of information flows. The library will become an important instrument in this development.

The main tasks of the library will continue to exist, such as ensuring effective information supply, and this includes the acquisition of information, providing technical assistance in the creation of new information by researchers, teachers and students and storing this information in a sustainable and accessible form. New tasks will have to be developed, such as information creation and tasks related to required technical competence, new interfaces and new service providers.

A strategic question is which services (computer services, databases, etc.) could and should be outsourced. Options are the institution's entire computing services, its e-mail services, its personnel administration, etc. An external service provider could possibly offer these services to several institutions in a more cost-effective way.

These strategic tasks will be the responsibility of an integrated information organisation embedded in the institution's research organisation. As stated above, it seems natural to utilise the expertise presently available at the library for the acquisition, dissemination and archiving of information, be this research, teaching or management information.

Service providers such as publishers and other players in the value chain

The observed and sketched developments in the scientific information market, in particular the convergence towards e-science, provide great opportunities for professional, commercial and non-commercial service providers. As we have seen, to grasp these opportunities it is important that these service providers develop a symbiotic relation with the research environment.

The present major international publishing houses enjoy a large market penetration in terms of published papers and financial potential that could well be used in a catalytic way. The active involvement of these publishers in the desired and required symbiotic relation would quickly lead to the establishment of necessary professional services that these new relations demand. This will lead to a broad discussion on the new demands of research and teaching and the use of new information instruments in these areas.

Other service providers will have opportunities to assume tasks to support the functioning of the overall network, such as in the areas of technical and administrative support. There is a special task in controlling the logistics of the network. As discussed before, the relation between publishers and other service providers such as agents requires review, and may lead to a tighter amalgamation of these service providers with the publishers; this may well be necessary to facilitate the necessary symbiotic relation of publishers with the research environment. This will therefore require further emancipation on the part of the publishers.

Strategy issues

Availability of and use of digital information are subject to a range of underlying legal arrangements, i.e. between the author of a work and the employer, the author of a work and its publisher and the institution that acquires a work from a publisher. Also the potential to network and integrate digital information owned or held by different institutions, authors and publishers will depend on the legal arrangements between the different stakeholders. Copyright law and contract law govern these legal arrangements, and differ from country to country.

The legal complexity of these arrangements calls for standardisation of the legal provisions between the various stakeholders. In the last few years several attempts at national and international levels have been made to this end. For instance, the copyright policies of institutions and ownership of copyright material have been discussed in a series of international working conferences called 'Copyright and Institutions: From Principles to Practices' organised by SURF in the Netherlands (the Zwolle Principles).[11]

As we have seen, basic information services (including peer review) can be separated from value-added services. This allows separating the protection of intellectual property as embedded in these basic services from the exploitation rights as commercially required for the value-added services. In particular, when repositories want to be successful in being accepted by researchers they are strongly recommended to offer researchers protection of intellectual property and against plagiarism. In this way, they will increase the chance of meeting their goal of attracting more material and providing broad availability of published material.

Some technical consequences

Research into the impact of the research modes on the use of scientific information will involve technological information developments such as reusable knowledge modules, middleware, durability, retrievability, search agents representing research profiles, editorial research and scientometric or bibliometric research (Roosendaal, 1995), to name just a few aspects. With respect to the latter, it is expected that digital storage and dissemination will add new dimensions and give new dynamics to scientometric or bibliometric research.

With respect to the archiving function, conditions for transparency need to be further explored. To implement the vision of new technical support for federated services, sources and computers, a new generation of middleware software is required at different levels:

- the technical level of federating and using heterogeneously distributed hardware
- implementation of exchange protocols and functions for import/export of services
- technical search and find functions in heterogeneous and distributed sources
- intelligent usage of collected information
- networking of content of worldwide but closely related institutions in a uniform interface
- integration from the user's view of competing heterogeneous service offers
- workflow for the certification and refereeing of information from distributed sources
- time-sensitive services such as managing institution-wide teaching schedules, meetings, conferences, worldwide 'distributed author collaboratories' and online discussions.

Technically, these middleware services can be implemented smoothly (Borghoff et al., 1997). However, this can only happen if there is a clear and agreed concept of future structures.

Future research

Research issues that emerge from the above are related to the discussed integration of stakeholders with the research environment. Further research is needed to develop a more detailed understanding of the possible relations between the stakeholders in such a future market, and the applicability of a virtual organisation as a model for the symbiotic relation described above between the research environment and the intermediaries.

With respect to developing a clearer understanding of the relations between the stakeholders, taking the perspective in this book of an alliance and applying strategic management knowledge of such alliances seems promising, in particular as it ensures a fully reflexive, combined outside-in and inside-out view. Utilising the two dimensions of organisational autonomy and strategic interdependence, and operationalising these dimensions for various levels of required integration, will allow the development of a more comprehensive understanding.

With respect to functions, the emphasis of future e-research should clearly be on certification and awareness, as these are decisive for the applicability of research results in the wider environment. In developing these functions further, proper attention should be paid to the different modes under which research is taking place, as this will influence these functions.

Notes

1 SCOAP3 (Sponsoring Consortium for Open Access Publishing in Particle Physics), www.scoap3.org.
2 Hochschulrektorenkonferenz (German Rectors Conference), www.hrk.de/.
3 Wissenschaftliche Literaturversorgungs- und Informations-systeme (LIS), German Research Foundation (DFG), www.dfg.de/forschungsfoerderung/wissenschaftliche _infrastruktur/lis/.
4 Dare Project, SURF, www.surffoundation.nl/en/themas/ wetenschappelijkecommunicatie/onderzoeksrepositoriesdare/ Pages/Default.aspx.
5 See the Research Councils UK position on the issue of improved access to research outputs, www.rcuk.ac.uk/access/ default.htm.
6 The text of the opt-out open access motion of Harvard Law School can be found at http://cyber.law.harvard.edu/node/ 4273.
7 Wellcome Trust open and unrestricted access to the outputs of published research, www.wellcome.ac.uk/About-us/Policy/ Spotlight-issues/Open-access/index.htm.
8 Berlin Declaration on Open Access to Knowledge in the Sciences and Humanities, made at Conference on Open Access to Knowledge in the Sciences and Humanities, Berlin, 20–22 October 2003, www.zim.mpg.de/openaccess-berlin/ berlindeclaration.html.
9 Open Archives Initiative, www.openarchives.org.
10 Archives of Open URL, OCLC, www.library.caltech.edu/ openurl/.
11 Copyright Management for Scholarship, SURF, http:// copyright.surf.nl/copyright/.

9

Summary and conclusions

The starting point in this book is that scientific information is here to serve researchers in producing scientific knowledge. This means serving researchers in making scientific results public and in acquiring scientific information.

Following this line of thinking, and using the concept of the business model as guidance to analyse the research environment, the competition and the drivers in research for making research results public and acquisition of these results by other researchers, we have first provided a discussion of research. We have analysed the scientific information market further from the viewpoint of a development towards e-science, as this opens up new possibilities for sharing information. Sharing information has been seen to be the main value proposition in the business model – the main purpose of scientific information – in particular when collaborating in research projects across institutions. E-science will create new challenges for smaller and medium-sized institutions in participating in such collaborations. E-science promises new possibilities for the production of knowledge, and will most probably change our research agenda in the future.

This research agenda is seen to be determined by the relation between research and society at large. This relation is presently in flux, moving towards an increasing intertwinement of research and society. The basic premise in the relation between society and researchers is that it should create incentives for both parties. As has been seen, scientific research is of interest not only to researchers but also to their societal environment. This societal environment plays a major role in setting research policies and directions. In setting research directions, this environment has a direct impact on scientific knowledge production.

We have analysed the strategic positioning of researchers in the environment, with an eye to the consequences this position has for the researchers' demands with respect to scientific information. In analysing strategic positioning, we have viewed the relation of researchers with the environment as a sort of alliance, allowing us to use concepts of the existing strategic management literature. In particular, we have used the two dimensions of organisational autonomy and strategic interdependence in analysing this strategic positioning. This approach is different from that usually taken in research policy literature, in that it not only allows an outside-in view, as is generally the view in research policy studies, but also allows an inside-out view, taking into account the unique resources and competencies of researchers, be these at the individual, research group or research institute level. This description leads to a continuum of modes of relations between researchers and the environment. Well-known modes are the 'ivory tower' and 'strategic research', known also as Mode1 and Mode2, and the recently introduced Mode3, the 'research entrepreneur'. These different modes lead to different demands for scientific information, in terms of both making results public and acquiring scientific information. As any business model in scientific publishing should serve researchers in their strategic positioning in the environment and in claiming the intellectual property of an invention, it is therefore argued that any business model should duly take into account these different demands of researchers. Competition has been seen to play a role here, in that it drives researchers to create new results, triggers innovative changes and drives researchers to make these results public. And indeed, researchers can withhold scientific results in order to gain competitive advantage over their colleagues by not sharing this information homogeneously throughout the research community, in this way hampering the integrity of science. Competition between researchers creates demand for the acquisition of information, in that it calls for selection tools to monitor and anticipate what research competitors intend.

The role of strategic positioning in the acquisition of scientific information has been illustrated by an extensive case study of a research institute, the MESA+ Institute for Nanotechnology at the University of Twente. The results show a spread over the different modes in positioning, although the researchers are predominantly located in Mode3, the research entrepreneur, and Mode2, the strategic researcher. This is also reflected in the observed motives to publish, which are spread over combinations of the three main motives of recognition, sharing knowledge and external pressure. Sharing knowledge was perceived as somewhat idealistic or even naïve as a motive, and occurs only in combination with one of the other two motives. In choosing a publication outlet, prestige, impact factor and the specific audience are therefore overriding factors.

The market for scientific communication has been analysed in terms of the forces driving this market and the functions it should perform. Although it is currently tempting to turn to technological forces driving the market, we have chosen forces and functions that are invariant in technological change. This approach is consistent with the position taken in this book that scientific information should serve researchers and therefore should take researchers as the pivotal point in the analysis, requiring forces and functions expressing the basic requirements of researchers independent of technology. Technology is enabling these requirements on the basis of the most up-to-date options. In this vein, and based on the analysis of the strategic positioning of researchers, we arrive at four forces driving the scientific information market: recognition of researchers, competition between researchers within both the research environment and the wider societal environment, and availability and selection of information. Following similar arguments, we arrive at the functions to be performed in the market: internal functions of certification and awareness, and external functions of registration and archiving.

This description of the market and its functions provides a consistent outline of the main forces in the market required to generate knowledge. The forces and functions together provide a useful description of the dynamics of the market as a whole, or the value created in the market. We have limited our discussion to the strategic positioning of researchers in operationalising the forces, and have discussed the four functions from the viewpoint of changes that could be anticipated from the further continuous development towards e-science. The certification function has been found to depend on the modes of strategic positioning of researchers. The specific research mode influences the authors' choice of a specific style of certification in the combination of content and potential application of the research being reported. A higher necessity for autonomy of researchers is connected to a stronger emphasis on the methodological aspects of certification, while a higher necessity for interdependence is connected to a stronger emphasis on the application aspects of certification. This results in a deliberate choice of certain journals deemed to have the right philosophy and style of reviewing research papers commensurate with the research mode. Journal editors are therefore advised to cater for the intended research mode as well as the intended market segment, and consequently for the right visibility and recognition for their clientele, the researchers, as there exists in particular a strong relation between intellectual property and the referee system.

The awareness function has been seen potentially to benefit from technological developments in terms of a wide array of value-added services aimed at increasing the selection of the reader, both in the development of communicating research results and in creating new landmarks alerting the researcher to material of interest. The aim is foremost to find all relevant information, and this still seems far away.

Next to certification, the registration function is most important for the author to claim intellectual property of the research results. Coupled to registration is protection of the intellectual ownership of these results. Important questions still to be solved in making the breakthrough to genuine modular publications are reliable authentication and timestamping, as well as encryption to ensure the integrity of the information.

The archiving function should ensure the sustainable deposit of material and its precise retrieval. A major problem in this arena is that the evolution of software, however necessary and positive this is in itself, makes existing information carriers and formats obsolete and thereby practically unusable, rendering the claim of archiving for posterity a hollow one. A way out for long-term archiving may be the strict logical separation of content and format, and strict usage of non-proprietary formats for the rather complex digital information products that this market requires. Neither the technological nor the organisational problems of how to distribute the material safely over a number of archives to create sustainable digital archives have been solved, but the necessary regulations, organisational structures and international agreements have been condensed into expertise for a national policy of long-term archiving of scientific documents. The essential obstacle on the way to a federated global document information system is the missing policy for the archiving and posting of data, and for document providers.

Bringing these elements together, we were able to formulate criteria for business models in scientific publishing by analysing the different elements in the business model: the value proposition, the market segment, the strategic position of researchers, the value chain of scientific publishing, including stakeholders such as libraries, publishers and other intermediaries, the competitive strategy, the potential for revenues and the cost structure.

The value proposition of the market is to serve the production of knowledge by sharing information: making research results public and acquiring information at the right time. The main property in the market is the intellectual property researchers claim when making results public. As the essence of a business model is the organisation of protection of the researchers' intellectual property, this is seen to be at the core of the value proposition. Sharing of knowledge can only be achieved through adequate availability of information.

The market segment has been shown to be not only the research environment worldwide but also the wider societal environment. Which market segment is most appropriate depends on the mode of strategic positioning of the researcher, as this mode determines what type of scientific information is required, acquired and produced.

The value chain derives from the forces and functions in the market in describing the dynamics in the market as a whole, and in this way the value in the market.

Competition in research is reflected in claiming intellectual property and thus creating competitive advantage for the owner of this property. But the acquisition of information also carries a competitive element. Effective acquisition requires powerful selection tools in the hands of the reader at the individual level. It then involves the researchers' choice of these tools in terms of value-added services. A business model should provide a proper balance between availability and selection at the researcher's discretion.

The revenue and cost structure depends on the two dimensions of availability and selection, as presented in the business model. A further requirement, and not the least, of the business model for scientific information is that it should be sustainable. A subsidised system could be considered, supported e.g. by research, but it should be noted that such a subsidised and therefore political system would possibly not only render the publishing system very vulnerable but could also endanger independent certification of research results, in this way endangering the research process itself.

The core of any scientific publishing business model is its ability to further the production of knowledge by sharing research results in an appropriate way. Core to sharing is the concomitant claim to and protection of the intellectual property of the researcher, and core to the validity of this claim is the certification function or the peer-review process.

In developing scenarios, we have noted that any publishing business model should be concerned with a proper balance between the two indispensable parameters of availability and ability to select. We have also noted that publishing involves the basic services (including peer review) on the one hand and enhanced power of selection on the other. These are two distinct services which can in principle be provided by separate suppliers: one responsible for wide availability of scientific information and one for value-added services, such as facilities to enhance the power of selection by researchers. In this way, a publishing business model can allow different combinations of availability and power of selection. This leads to a suite of different business models for scientific publishing in which availability and selection can in principle be provided by different combinations of suppliers. Responsibilities and costs for availability can be kept separate from responsibilities and costs for selection. These models allow researchers to acquire selected information and choose services for which they want to pay additionally.

The way availability and selection are arranged in the present market has been demonstrated using the subscription model and the open access model. Furthermore, based on the observation that in principle basic services can be split from value-added services, a suite of optional business models have been proposed meeting this requirement of flexible separation. It can be concluded that only such a demand-oriented and research-centred model providing basic services combined with optional added-value services meets the conditions for scientific information as demanded by the research community, taking all elements of the business model into account. Many business models meeting these general conditions will be possible, allowing a much richer market than the present situation of one dominant business model. Rather than listing all possible business models, we have chosen in this book to restrict ourselves to conditions for such models.

Inspecting the current dominant business model, the subscription model, it was shown that this is a supply-oriented and publisher-centred model. The open access model in all its variations present in the market was seen to be in essence also a supply-oriented and publisher-centred model. This means that neither of these models meets the demands of convergence in the scientific information market towards e-science, which was shown to require a demand-oriented and research-centred business model.

Any business model should comply with the prime demand of research for sharing scientific information for the benefit of researchers, i.e. sharing information in a very dynamic environment demanding that information must be made public and can be fully acquired. Such a business model leads to a network comprising the research environment as the pivotal stakeholder together with other stakeholders. This network requires careful strategic positioning of these other stakeholders with respect to the research environment. The analysis then arrives at the conclusion that libraries can best be absorbed into research, like in the Cochrane Library, whereas with publishers and other intermediaries a symbiotic relation should be established to guarantee a sustainable business model. The relation between publishers and other service providers needs revision and may lead to a tighter amalgamation of these parties. This will therefore require further emancipation on the part of the publishers.

The creation of a cohesive and coherent network should allow and guarantee the best return on investment, in whatever form, for all stakeholders on their own terms, be they public organisations such as research and higher education institutions or private organisations such as publishers. It is in the interest of each individual stakeholder to strive for maximum flexibility in the marketplace. This can best be achieved by organising the market in such a way that it allows maximum compliance with the vision in the marketplace.

The guiding thought throughout this book is that scientific publishing is here to serve scientific knowledge production. Stimulating e-science is the challenge for scientific publishing. E-science means a further step in the integration of information into the research process, requiring new strategies and business models for scientific publishing.

This book has discussed some aspects of the new strategies and business models that are required to meet this goal of serving research.

References

All web links in these references and throughout the book were checked and found to be working on 24 May 2009. All links given here and throughout the book can be accessed online at http://www.isn-oldenburg.de/~hilf/publications/scientific-publishing-from-vanity-to-strategy.html, *which page will be regularly checked and updated by the authors.*

Altbach, P.G. (ed.) (1996) *The International Academic Profession*. Princeton, NJ: Carnegie Foundation for Advancement of Teaching.

Amit, R. and Zott, C. (2001) 'Value creation in e-business', *Strategic Management Journal*, 22(6/7): 493–520.

Baeza-Yates, R. and Ribeiro-Neto, B. (1999) *Modern Information Retrieval*. New York: ACM Press/Addison-Wesley.

Barnes, D. (1987) 'Meeting on AIDS drugs turns into open forum', *Science: New Series, News and Comments*, 4820: 1287–8.

Borghoff, U.M., Hilf, E.R., Pareschi, R., Severiens, T., Stamerjohanns, H. and Willamowski, J. (1997) 'Agent-based document retrieval for the European physicists: a project overview', paper presented at Practical Applications of Intelligent Agents and Multi-Agents (PAAM '97), London, 21–23 April; available at: *www.physik.uni-oldenburg.de/documents/UOL-THEO-97-3/*.

Brown, C. (1999) 'Information seeking behavior of scientists in the electronic information age: astronomers, chemists, mathematicians and physicists', *Journal of the American Society for Information Science*, 50(10): 929–43.

Campbell, E.G. and Blumenthal, D. (2002) 'The selfish gene: data sharing and withholding in academic genetics', *Science (Science Careers)*, 31 May.

Campbell, E.G., Wiessman, J.S., Causino, N. and Blumenthal, D. (2000) 'Data withholding in academic medicine: characteristics of faculty denied access to research results and biomaterials', *Research Policy*, 29: 303–12.

Ceci, S.J. (1998) 'Scientists' attitudes toward data sharing', *Science, Technology & Human Values*, 13(1/2): 45–52.

Chesbrough, H. and Rosenbloom, R.S. (2002) 'The role of the business model in capturing value from innovation: evidence from Xerox Corporation's technology spin-offs companies', *Industrial and Corporate Change*, 11(3): 529–55.

Clark, B. (2001) 'The entrepreneurial university: new foundations for collegiality, autonomy, and achievement', *Higher Education Management*, 13(2): 9–24.

Collins, R. (1968) 'Competition and social control in science: an essay in theory-construction', *Sociology of Education*, 41(2): 123–40.

Cope, B. and Philips, A. (eds) (2006) *The Future of the Book in the Digital Age*. Oxford: Chandos Publishing.

Cope, B. and Philips, A. (eds) (2009) *The Future of the Academic Journal*. Oxford: Chandos Publishing.

Daniel, H.D. (1993) *Guardians of Science: Fairness and Reliability of Peer Review*. Weinheim: VCH.

Davis, P.M. (2004) 'Information-seeking behavior of chemists: a transaction log analysis of referral URLs',

Journal of the American Society for Information Science and Technology, 55(4): 326–32.

de Guchteneire, Paul (2004) *Code of Conduct for Social Science Research*. Paris: UNESCO.

de Jong, H. and Rip, A. (1997) 'The computer revolution in science: steps towards the realization of computer-supported discovery environments', *Artificial Intelligence*, 91: 225–56.

de Jong, H. and van Raalte, F. (1999) 'Comparative envisionment construction', *Artificial Intelligence*, 115: 145–214.

de Jong, H., Mars, N.J.I. and van der Vet, P.E. (1999) 'Computer-supported resolution of measurement conflicts: a case-study in materials science', *Foundations of Science*, 4: 427–61.

de Rosnay, Melanie Dulong (2008) 'Harvard goes open access', Berkman Center for Internet and Society; available at: *http://cyber.law.harvard.edu/node/3462*.

de Solla Price, D.J. (1986) *Little Science, Big Science… and Beyond*. New York: Columbia University Press.

den Braber, Maarten (2008) 'Rethinking the hospital', master's thesis, University of Twente.

DINI-Zertifikat (2007) 'Workgroup on electronic publishing', Document and Publication Service, Deutsche Initiative für NetzwerkInformation; available at: *www.dini.de/fileadmin/docs/dini_zertifikat_2007_v2.1.pdf*.

Euzenat, J. (1995) 'Building consensual knowledge bases: context and architecture', in N.J.I. Mars (ed.) *Towards Very Large Knowledge Bases*. Amsterdam: IOS Press, pp. 143–55.

Frederiksson, E.H. (ed.) (2001) *A Century of Science Publishing*. Amsterdam: IOS Press.

Gaston, J. (1970) 'The reward system in British science', *American Sociological Review*, 35(4): 718–32.

Gaston, J. (1973) *Originality and Competition in Science. A Study of the British High Energy Physics Community.* London: University of Chicago Press.

Gaston, J. (1978) *The Reward System in British and American Science.* New York: John Wiley & Sons.

Geurts, Peter A.Th.M. and Roosendaal, Hans E. (2001) 'Estimating the direction of innovative change based on theory and mixed methods', *Quality & Quantity*, 35: 407–27.

Gibbons, M. (1999) 'Science's new social contract with society', *Nature*, 402: C81–4.

Gibbons, M., Limoges, C., Novotny, H., Schwartzman, S., Scott, P. and Trow, M. (1994) *The New Production of Knowledge. The Dynamics of Science and Research in Contemporary Societies.* Stockholm: Sage Publications.

Gross, A.G. (1994) *The Rhetoric of Science.* Cambridge, MA: Harvard University Press.

Hagstrom, W.O. (1965) *The Scientific Community.* New York: Basic Books.

Hagstrom, W.O. (1974) 'Competition in science', *American Sociological Review*, 29(1): 1–18.

Haspeslagh, P.C. and Jemison, D.B. (1991) *Managing Acquisitions. Creating Value through Corporate Renewal.* New York: Free Press.

Hearst, M. (1997) 'Interfaces for searching the web', *Scientific American*, March, pp. 60–4.

Heimeriks, G. and Vasileiadou, E. (2008) 'Changes or transition? Analysing the use of ICTs in the sciences', *Social Science Information*, 47(1): 5–29.

Hilf, Eberhard R. (2002a) 'Verfassung für den Umgang mit Information in den Wissenschaften – Besonderheiten, Beispiele, Handlungsbedarf der Politik', paper presented at WissensWert, das Internet und die neue

Wissensordnung, Berlin, 17–18 April; available at: *www.isn-oldenburg.de/~hilf/vortraege/wissenswert/*.

Hilf, Eberhard R. (2002b) 'Copyright, Urheberrecht und die Anforderungen der Wissenschaften', paper presented at DINI Brainstorm Session, Göttingen, 27 November; available at: *www.isn-oldenburg.de/~hilf/vortraege/dini-copy02/*.

Hilf, Eberhard R. and Mimkes, Julika (2002) 'Metadaten, Nachweis und Nutzung von E-Learning', in DINI-Jahrestagung, *Anforderungen durch E-Learning*, Dresden; available at: *www.tu-dresden.de/t2002/hilf/dresden02-neu.html*.

Hilf, Eberhard R. and Wätjen, Hans-Joachim (2001) 'Publishing and refereeing in a distributed world – the views of a physicist and a librarian', paper presented at LIBER Workshop on the Open Archives Initiative (OAI) and Peer Review Journals in Europe, Geneva, 22–24 March; available at: *http://eprints.rclis.org/909/3/hilf_waetjen_genf2.pdf* and *www.isn-oldenburg.de/~hilf/vortraege/cern01*.

Hilf, Eberhard R., Kappenberg, Bernd and Roosendaal Hans E. (2008) 'Author identification: the benefit of being able to identify researchers uniquely', *The Euroscientist*, 5; available at: *www.euroscience.org/*.

Hodgkinson. G. (ed.) (2001) 'Bridging the relevance gap', *British Journal of Management*, 12(1), special issue.

Hummels, Harry and Roosendaal, Hans E. (2001) 'Trust in scientific publishing', *Journal of Business Ethics*, 34: 87–100.

Kahn, R.F. (1994) 'Deposit, registration and recordation in an electronic copyright management system', IMA Intellectual Property Project Proceedings; available at: *www.ifla.org/documents/infopol/copyright/kahn.txt*.

Kircz, Joost G. (1998) 'Modularity: the next form of scientific information presentation?', *Journal of Documentation*, 54(2): 210–35.

Kist, Joost (2008) *New Thinking for 21st Century Publishers*. Oxford: Chandos Publishing.

Knorr-Cetina, K.D. (1981) *The Manufacture of Knowledge: An Essay on the Constructivist and Contextual Nature of Science*. Oxford: Pergamon Press.

Kurek, Kasia, Geurts, Peter A.Th.M. and Roosendaal, Hans E. (2006) 'The split between availability and selection. Business models for scientific information, and the scientific process?', *Information Services & Use*, 26(4): 217–82.

Kurek, Kasia, Geurts, Peter A.Th.M. and Roosendaal, Hans E. (2007) 'The research entrepreneur: strategic positioning of the researcher in his societal environment', *Science and Public Policy*, 34(7): 501–13.

Latour, Bruno (1987) *Science in Action, How to Follow Scientists and Engineers through Society*. Cambridge, MA: Harvard University Press.

Laudel, G. (2006) 'The art of getting funded: how scientists adapt to their funding conditions', *Science and Public Policy*, 33(7): 489–504.

Leydesdorff, L. and Etzkowitz, H. (1998) 'Triple helix of innovation: introduction', *Science and Public Policy*, 25(6): 358–64.

Leydesdorff, L. and Meyer, M. (eds) (2006) 'Triple helix indicators of knowledge-based innovation systems', *Research Policy*, 35(10): 1441–674.

Maddox, J.R. (1998) *What Remains to Be Discovered*. New York: Free Press.

Magretta, J. (2002) 'Why business models matter', *Harvard Business Review*, 80(5): 86–92.

Mäkinen, S. and Seppänen, M. (2007) 'Assessing business model concepts with taxonomical research criteria', *Management Research News*, 30(10): 735–48.

McCain, K.W. (1991) 'Communication, competition, and secrecy: the production and dissemination of research-related information in genetics', *Science, Technology & Human Values*, 16(4): 491–516.

Meadows, A.J. (1998) *Communicating Research*. San Diego, CA: Academic Press.

Merton, R.K. (1957) 'Priorities in scientific discovery: a chapter in the sociology of science', *American Sociological Review*, 22: 635–59.

Merton, R.K. (1973) *The Sociology of Science: Theoretical and Empirical Investigations*. Chicago, IL, and London: University of Chicago Press.

National Science Foundation (2008) 'Federal funds, research and related activities', in *The Budget for Fiscal Year 2009*, General Fund Receipt Account. Arlington, VA: NSF, pp. 1091–6.

Netherlands Organisation for Scientific Research (2008) *NWO Annual Report 2007: Including Indicators of Accountability*. The Hague: NWO.

Nijholt, A., Hulstijn, J. and van Hessen, A. (1999) 'Speech and language interactions in a web theatre environment', in P. Dalsgaard, C.-H. Lee, P. Heisterkamp and R. Cole (eds) *Proceedings of the ESCA Workshop on Interaction Dialogue in Multi-Modal Systems*. Aalborg: ESCA/Center for PersonKommunikation, pp. 129–32.

Novotny, H., Scott, P. and Gibbons, M. (2003) 'Introduction: "Mode2" revisited: the new production of knowledge', *Minerva*, 41: 179–94.

Osterwalder, A., Pigneur, Y. and Tucci, C.L. (2005) 'Clarifying business models: origins, presence and future of the concept', *Communications of AIS*, 16: 1–25.

Popper, K. (1934) *Logik der Forschung: zur Erkenntnistheorie der modernen Naturwissenschaft.* Vienna: Springer.

Popper, K. (1959) *The Logic of Scientific Discovery.* London: Hutchinson & Co.

Popper, K. (1963) *Conjectures and Refutations: The Growth of Scientific Knowledge.* London: Routledge & Kegan Paul.

Prosser, D.C. (2005) 'The next information revolution – how open access will transform scholarly communication', in G.E. Gorman and F. Rowland (eds) *International Yearbook of Library and Information Management 2004–2005: Scholarly Publishing in an Electronic Era.* London: Facet Publishing, pp. 99–117; available at: *http://eprints.rclis.org/archive/00003917/.*

Roosendaal, Hans E. (1995) 'Roles of bibliometrics in scientific communication', invited talk at Fourth International Science and Technology Indicators Conference, Antwerp, 5–7 October, published in *Research Evaluation,* 5(3): 237–41.

Roosendaal, Hans E. (2004) 'Driving change in the research and HE information market', *Learned Publishing,* 17(1): 11–16.

Roosendaal, Hans E. and de Ruiter, A.P. (1990) 'The journal at the crossroads of developments in scientific information and information technology', paper presented at conference in Helsinki.

Roosendaal, Hans E. and Geurts, Peter A.Th.M. (1997) 'Forces and functions in scientific communication: an analysis of their interplay', in *Proceedings of the Conference on Co-operative Research in Information Systems in Physics,* University of Oldenburg, Germany; available at: *www.physik.uni-oldenburg.de/conferences/ crisp97/roosendaal.html.*

Roosendaal, Hans E. and Geurts, Peter A.Th.M. (1999) 'Scientific communication and its relevance to research policy', *Scientometrics*, 44(3): 507–19.

Roosendaal, Hans E., Geurts, Peter A.Th.M. and Hilf, Eberhard R. (2005) 'Pertinent strategy issues in scientific information and communication in 2004', invited review in Petra Hauke (ed.) *Library Science – Quo Vadis?*, Institute of Library Science at the Humboldt University Berlin. Munich: K.G. Saur Verlag, pp. 217–38.

Roosendaal, Hans E., Geurts, Peter A.Th.M. and van der Vet, Paul E. (2001a) 'Developments in scientific communication: considerations on the value chain', *Information Services and Use*, 21:13–32.

Roosendaal, Hans E., Geurts, Peter A.Th.M. and van der Vet, Paul E. (2001b) 'Developments in scientific communication – the virtual marketplace as a prerequisite for growth', in E.H. Frederiksson (ed.) *A Century of Science Publishing*. Amsterdam: IOS Press.

Roosendaal, Hans E., Geurts, Peter A.Th.M. and van der Vet, Paul E. (2001c) 'Higher education needs may determine the future of scientific publishing', *Nature*; available at: *www.nature.com/nature.debates/e-access/Articles/roosendaal.html*.

Roosendaal, Hans E., Geurts, Peter A.Th.M. and van der Vet, Paul E. (2002a) 'Eine neue Wertschöpfungskette für den Markt der wissenschaftlichen Information?', *Bibliothek Forschung und Praxis*, 26(2): 149–53; available at: *www.bibliothek-saur.de/preprint/2002/roosenda_end.pdf*.

Roosendaal, Hans E., Geurts, Peter A.Th.M. and van der Vet, Paul E. (2002b) 'Integration of information for research and education: changes in the value chain?', *Serials*, 15(1): 51–6.

Roosendaal, Hans E., Kurek, Kasia and Geurts, Peter A.Th.M. (2008) 'Modèles économiques de l'édition scientifique et processus de recherche', in J. Schöpfel (ed.) *La publication scientifique. Analyses et perspectives.* Lavoisier: Hermes Science.

Roosendaal, Hans E., Huibers, Theo W.C., Geurts, Peter A.Th.M. and van der Vet, Paul E. (2003) 'Changes in the value chain of scientific information: economic consequences for academic institutions', *Online Information Review*, 27: 120–8.

Rothenberg, Jeff (2000) 'Using emulation to preserve digital documents', *NELiNET*, 5 June; available at: *www. nelinet.net/edserv/conf/digital/dr_2000/rothen2.pdf.*

Schöpfel, J. (2008) *La publication scientifique. Analyses et perspectives.* Lavoisier: Hermes Science.

Schwander, T. (2002) 'TeX als Archivierungssprache', paper presented at MathDissInternational Workshop, Staats- und Universitätsbibliothek Göttingen; available at: *www.ub.uni-duisburg.de/mathdiss/Schwander/ vortrag.html.*

Severiens, Thomas (2008) 'Requirements for author registries', *The Euroscientist*, 5; available at: *www. euroscience.org/.*

Severiens, Thomas and Hilf, E.R. (2006a) 'Langzeit-archivierung von Rohdaten', *Nestor-materialien*, 6; available at: *http://edoc.hu-berlin.de/series/nestor-materialien/6/PDF/6.pdf* and *www.langzeitarchivierung.de.*

Severiens, Thomas and Hilf, E.R. (2006b) 'Zur Entwicklung eines Beschreibungsprofils für eine nationale Langzeit-Archivierungs-Strategie – ein Beitrag aus der Sicht der Wissenschaften', *Nestor-materialien*, 7; available at: *www.langzeitarchivierung.de/downloads/mat/nestor_ mat_07.pdf.*

Shafer, S.M., Smith, H.J. and Linder, J.C. (2005) 'The power of business models', *Business Horizons*, 48(3): 199–207.

Sparck Jones, K. (1998) 'Summary performance comparisons: TREC-2, TREC-3, TREC-4, TREC-5, TREC-6', in E.M. Voorhees and D.K. Harman (eds) *The Sixth Text Retrieval Conference (TREC-6)*. Gaithersburg, MD: US Department of Commerce, National Institute of Standards and Technology, pp. B-1–8.

Swan, J., Robertson, M., Newell, S., Dopson, S. and Bresnen, M. (2007) 'When policy meets practice – the problems of "Mode2" initiatives in the translation of academic knowledge', paper presented at Third Organization Studies Summer Workshop: Generation and Use of Academic Knowledge about Organizations, Crete, 7–9 June.

Tenopir, C. and King, D. (2000) *Towards Electronic Journals: Realities for Scientists, Librarians and Publishers*. Washington, DC: Special Libraries Association.

van der Vet, P.E. (2000) 'Building web resources for natural scientists', in H. Scholten and M.J. van Sinderen (eds) *Interactive Distributed Multimedia Systems and Telecommunication Services*. Berlin: Springer, pp. 205–10.

van der Vet, P.E. and Mars, N.J.I. (1999) 'CQE: a query engine for coordinated index terms', *Journal of the American Society for Information Science*, 50: 485–92.

Vatcheva, I. and de Jong, H. (1999) 'Semi-quantitative comparative analysis', in T.D. Dean (ed.) *Proceedings of the Sixteenth International Joint Conference on Artificial Intelligence, IJCAI-99*. San Francisco, CA: Morgan Kaufmann, pp. 1034–40.

Wadman, M. (1996) 'Commercial interests delay publication', *Nature*, 379(6566): 574.

Wayt Gibbs, W. (2000) 'How Publius thwarts censors', *Scientific American*, October, pp. 23–4.

Wilts, A. (2000) 'Forms of research organisation and their responsiveness to external goal setting', *Research Policy*, 29: 767–81.

Yoxen, E. (1988) 'Public concern and the steering of science. Report for the Science Policy Support Group', University of Manchester, Department of Science and Technology Policy. London: SPSG.

Zalewska-Kurek, Kasia (2008) 'Strategies in the production and dissemination of knowledge', PhD dissertation, University of Twente.

Zalewska-Kurek, Kasia, Geurts, Peter A.Th.M. and Roosendaal, Hans E. (2008) 'The use of business models for scientific publishing in the production of knowledge', in Kasia Zalewska-Kurek, 'Strategies in the production and dissemination of knowledge', PhD dissertation, University of Twente, pp. 105–21.

Ziman, J. (1994) *Prometheus Bound. Science in a Dynamic Steady State*. Cambridge: Cambridge University Press.

Zinn-Justin, J. (1997) 'Peer review and electronic publishing', invited talk at CRISP '97, Oldenburg, 31 August–4 September; available at: *http://www.physics.mcgill.ca/_karttune/crisp97/*.

Index

Printed and bound by CPI Group (UK) Ltd, Croydon, CR0 4YY

08/05/2025

01864969-0003